THE SWORD
IN THE
AGE OF CHIVALRY

THE SWORD
IN THE
AGE OF CHIVALRY

Ewart Oakeshott

with drawings by the author

THE BOYDELL PRESS

First published 1964

Reissued 1994
The Boydell Press, Woodbridge
Reprinted 1995
Reprinted in paperback 1998, 2002

Transferred to digital printing 2009

ISBN 978-0-85115-715-3

The Boydell Press is an imprint of Boydell & Brewer Ltd
PO Box 9, Woodbridge, Suffolk IP12 3DF, UK
and of Boydell & Brewer Inc.
668 Mt. Hope Avenue, Rochester NY 14620, USA
website: www.boydellandbrewer.com

A CIP catalogue record for this title is available
from the British Library

This book is printed on acid-free paper

Printed in Great Britain by
4edge Ltd, Hockley, Essex

Contents

Preface to the 1994 Edition

THIS book, having been prepared and published in the early 1960s, contains many errors in the matter of the dating of swords. Since then, thirty more years of thought based upon many significant archaeological finds have exposed these errors. My publishers and I have decided not to amend the actual text, but rather to add an appendix wherein these errors are corrected. Further finds and more study will inevitably bring about the need for yet further amendments. Any publication of archaeological research must always be subject to the possibility of new evidence calling for a change of mind, and for any true scholar this must demand an admission of error. To avoid confusion, I ask my readers to refer constantly to this appendix because all of these reassessments, and all of this fresh thought have appeared in my *Records of the Medieval Sword* (Boydell Press, 1991).

Those of my readers who are already familiar with my work will know that I write in a conversational style. I believe that a person-to-person approach is more likely to be appreciated by those for whom I write, than a strictly academic one. I am not, nor ever have been, an "expert", and I will not write merely for the benefit of experts. The words "amateur" and "dilettante" have become pejorative. An amateur is held to be a person of no consequence who interferes with matters which he does not understand, while a dilettante is considered to be a human butterfly who flits with frivolous insouciance from one enthusiasm to another. But to be referred to as "a renaissance man" is considered (and rightly so) to be a great compliment, and yet all three of these expressions mean (or used to mean) the same thing. The amateur, the lover of his subject, is one who does not follow only the particular and narrow discipline in which he works – that is the function of the expert – but encourages his attention to stretch away into the study of any or every thing even remotely connected with it. That, too, is what the true dilettante must do. In the case of the study of armour and arms, and of their corollary, the ethics of elegant combat, a constant study of history is basic. It is also necessary to be able to practise what is preached.

Long ago – more than fifty years ago – I found that in order to do justice to a real study of the sword, not just to have a love-affair with it, I had to wander off into fascinating by-ways; it was essential of course to study not only the history of the period, but its art, and not only its art, but its literature – all of it, from saga, chronicle, will and inventory to love poems and pub songs and other frivolities. These things, and only these things, can give some understanding of the *Zeitgeist* of a period without which there can be no true appreciation of a sword or a war-harness, or indeed of anything else.

These by-ways, which always led back to the main road, took me far away from England, for most of the material I needed came from Europe and Asia – from Ireland to Siberia and from Finland to Andalusia. I also had to learn how to wear armour and ride in it, and to heft the sword. These splendid things are not simply ancient artifacts buried in the ground of times past, to be dug up for the benefit of the egos of 20th century experts. They were objects of everyday use by real, very simple people – objects also of mystery and veneration.

So: I am indeed an amateur, whose aim is to arouse the interest of any person who cares to read what I write, to be helpful to the student of history or culture or art, and to increase the pleasure of those who collect these splendid things – and now, in these days, of all those who so eagerly and skilfully use them in combat.

When this book was in preparation in 1962, I wrote a preface in which I acknowledged my indebtedness to several eminent authorities, working in the field of arms and armour studies, for their support and encouragement. Thirty-two years on, those personages belong to history and there is little point in reiterating this acknowledgement but if, now, I were to try to thank by name all those who support me, a mere preface would be totally inadequate. So I make a general, wide-ranging expression of deep gratitude to all who may read this, wherever they may be, all over the world. It is to them – to you – that I owe the will and the ability to go on working in this most fascinating field of study as my eightieth year rapidly approaches; and it is for you I write. Without the warmth and appreciation of so many people – some close and dear friends, some interesting acquaintances to whom I hope to get closer, and some known to me only by their letters – I would be a spent force.

So thirty years on I do not make acknowledgements to great authorities of the past, but I say thank you, to all of you who still regard my work as useful, and without whose encouragement I could no longer function.

List of Plates

13. Type XIIIa, I, 5. ?S. German, c. 1260–1300 (*Author's Collection*).
14. A. Type XIIIa, c. 1280–1310 (*Burrell Collection, Glasgow*). B. Type XIIIa (*Burrell Collection, Glasgow, ex. Morgan Williams and Martineau Collections*). C. Type XVa. Second half of the 14th century (*Collection, J. Pocock*).
15. Type XIV, J1, 4. Italian, first quarter of the 14th century (*Metropolitan Museum of Art, New York*).
16. Type XIV, J1, 4. Italian, first quarter of the 14th century (*Metropolitan Museum of Art, New York*).
17. Type XIIIb, I, 2. Spanish, before 1319. A small weapon made for a boy (*Cathedral Treasury of Toledo*).
18. Hilt of "Santa Casilda" sword (*Instituto del Conde Valencia de Don Juan, Madrid*).
19. Three types, all in use 1250–1325, contrasted. A. Type XIIIb; c. 1300 (*Wallace Collection, London*). B. Type XIV; c. 1300 (*Author's Collection*) (see plate 46B). C. Type XII (*Instituto del Conde de Valencia de Don Juan, Madrid*).
20. A. Type XIV. Early 14th century (*Collection, John Wallace, ex. Baron C. A. de Cosson*). B. Type XVI. First half of the 14th century (*National Museum, Copenhagen*). C. Type XIV (or XVI?) (*Collection, J. Pocock*).
21. Hilt of sword of Estore Visconti, plate 22B (*Cathedral Treasury, Monza*).
22. A. Type XV, late 13th–early 14th century (*Wallace Collection, London*). B. Type XV. Early 15th century sword of Estore Visconti. C. Type XVIII. Mid-15th century (*Kunsthistorisches Museum, Vienna*).
23. Hilt, of gilt bronze with horn grip, of Type XV sword shown on plate 24 (*Metropolitan Museum of Art, New York*).
24. Type XV, J, 8 (curved). ?Italian, first half of the 15th century (*Metropolitan Museum of Art, New York*).
25. Type XV, J1, 10; c. 1400 (*Cambridge, Museum of Ethnology and Archaeology*).
26. A. Type XVI, early 14th century (*City Museum, Lincoln*). B. Falchion, early 14th century (*Castle Museum, Norwich*). C. Type XV (see plate 27A); c. 1400 (*Wallace Collection, London*). D. Scottish sword, vaguely of Type XVIII (*Collection, C. O. von Kienbusch, New York*).
27. A. Type XV; c. 1400 (*Wallace Collection, London*). B. Type XV. Second half of the 15th century (*Author's Collection*). C. Type XVa. Found in Lake Constance (*Collection, the late Sir Edward Barry, Bart.*).
28. Type XVIa. First half of the 14th century. A. Found in London (*British Museum*). B. *National Museum, Copenhagen*; C. *Burrell Collection, Glasgow, ex. Morgan Williams Collection.*
29. Type XVIa, K, Ia. First half of the 14th century (*H.M. Tower of London*).
30. Type XVII. A. Second half of 14th century (*Castel St. Angelo, Rome*). B. Second half of the 14th century (*Collection, E. A. Christensen*). C. Second half of the 14th century (*Bayerische National Museum, Munich*).
31. Hilt of plate 30C.
32. Hilt of plate 34.
33. A. Type XVIIIb, T4, 4; c. 1400 (*Collection, the late Sir James Mann*). B. Type XVIIIb, J1, 12. German, second half of the 15th century (*Bayerische National Museum, Munich*).
34. Type XVIII, J, 8. First quarter of the 15th century (*Metropolitan Museum of Art, New York*).

35. A. Second half of the 14th century (*Wallace Collection, London*) B. Type XVIII. Late 15th century. Made in Milan for the Archduke Philip the Handsome (*Kunsthistorisches Museum, Vienna*).
36. Type XVIIIa. A. ?Flemish, mid-15th century (*Wallace Collection, London*). B. Mid-15th century (*Author's Collection*).
37. Type XVIIIa, J, 11 (*Collection, E. A. Christensen, Copenhagen*).
38. Type XVIIIc, G, 5+. Spanish, last quarter of the 15th century (*Author's Collection*).
39. A. Type XIX, T1, 5 (*Royal Ontario Museum, Toronto*). B. Type XIX, G, 5+. Dated 1432 (*H.M. Tower of London*). C. Type XIX, G, 6+. Spanish, last quarter of the 15th century (*Instituto del Conde de Valencia de Don Juan, Madrid*).
40. Type XX. A. First quarter of the 14th century (*Waffensammlung, Vienna*). B. First quarter of the 14th century (*Collection, R. T. Gwynn*). C. Mid-14th century (*Collection, Claude Blair*).
41. Venetian sword, second half of the 15th century (*Collection, C. O. von Kienbusch, New York*).
42. Type XX. A. Ceremonial sword of the Emperor Frederic III, *c.* 1450 (*Waffensammlung, Vienna*). B. Sword of the Emperor Sigismund I, made in 1435 (*Waffensammlung, Vienna*). C. Sword with a very crudely-made hilt of horn, in cinquedea form (*ex. Collections W. Bashford Dean, D. Ash, and Author. Sold by Fischer of Lucerne, July 1964*).
43. A. Back-edged sword, early 14th century, with finger-ring (found in Italy. *Collection, G. Bini, Rome*). B. Type XVIII, first quarter of the 15th century. Cross (Style 2) with side ring (*Collection, David Drey, ex, Author's*). C. Type XIX. Spanish, last quarter of the 15th century. Developed ring-guards (*Castel Sant'Angelo, Rome*). D. Indeterminate type, of "Venetian" fashion. Mid-15th century (*Collection, C. O. von Kienbusch, New York*).
44. Type XX, late 15th century. A. Long blade with cinquedea hilt. B. Hilt of A (*Collection, David Drey, ex. de Cosson, D. Ash and Author's collections*). C. Type XXa. Small sword, possibly made for a boy (*Author's Collection*).
45. Hilt of plate 33B. Second half of the 15th century (*Bayerische National Museum, Munich*).
46. A. Type ?XIIIb, I, 2. Italian, early 14th century. Found in the coffin of Can Grande della Scala, +1329, Verona (*Museo Archaeologico, Verona*). B. Type XIV, K, 1a (curved). ?Italian, early 14th century (*Author's Collection*). C. Type XVIII, ?V, ?2. German, mid-15th century (*H.M. Tower of London*). D. Type XV, G1, 10. Italian, mid-15th century (*Author's Collection*).
47. Type XVIa, K, 5+. First half of the 14th century (*National Museum, Copenhagen*).
48. Contrasting styles of inlay on blades. A. 10th century, sword of Type X (*National Museum, Copenhagen*). B. First half of 10th century (*British Museum*). C. Second half of the 13th century, Type XII (*Victoria and Albert Museum*). D. Bladesmith's mark, enlarged 2–1. Sword of Type XIIIa, early 14th century (*National Museum, Copenhagen*).

Introduction

IT is a popular belief that the medieval sword was a weapon of unvarying (though vaguely defined) form, a crude chopping instrument intolerably heavy and clumsy, redolent of blood yet at the same time a symbol of much bogus romanticism. Until quite recently this unfortunate view was held even by some students and collectors of arms, and it is still kept alive by the comments of scholars and historians[1] (not to mention some writers of historical novels) who for reasons unconnected with any particular interest in the weapon itself state baldly that it was inefficient or excessively heavy or otherwise brutish and ineffectual. Such comment stems from lack of acquaintance with medieval swords, but coming (as it often does) from authoritative sources it can be very misleading.

This work is an attempt, made after a quarter-century of study of the European sword in the period A.D. 1100 to 1500, to present this splendid weapon in its true colours; and as the study has been practical as well as academic, the presentation will not be of the sword as a mere archaeological specimen, examined, analysed and pushed into a typological strait-jacket, but of a most noble weapon which once had high significance in the minds of men, and fulfilled the most vital and personal service in their hands.

It may be appropriate to start with an effort to analyse the erroneous popular view. Why have unnecessary misconceptions arisen? Primarily perhaps because of the rarity and inaccessibility of raw material for study. Among the great mass of military hardware which has survived there are very few items which date before the Renaissance. The only medieval swords the average man—one might add, the average collector—sees, are black and corroded relics behind glass in museums. Such excavated examples bear about as much relation to "living" swords in pristine condi-

[1] Even Sir Steven Runciman in his monumental work on the Crusades.

II

tion as the rotting ribs of a wreck thrusting up from estuarial mud bear to the ship they were once part of. Such battered objects, seen but not handled or understood, may well give an impression of crudity. Add to this the work of romantic writers in the past, who, seeking to give to their heroes a touch of the Superman, caused them to wield enormous and weighty weapons far beyond the powers of modern man, and complete the picture with the scorn poured upon these swords by lovers of the elegance of the 18th century, or of the robust glamour of the Elizabethan era and the glories of Renaissance art,[2] and it becomes easier to see why so plain a weapon, seen only in a decayed state, can be accounted crude, ponderous and inefficient. Of course there are always those to whom simple austerity of form is indistinguishable from crudity; and an iron object a yard long may well appear to be very heavy. In fact the average weight of these swords is between 2 lbs. and 3 lbs., and they were balanced (according to their purpose) with the same care and skill in the making as a tennis racket or a fishing-rod. The old belief that they are unwieldable is as absurd and out-dated, and dies as hard, as the myth that armoured knights had to be hoisted into their saddles with a crane.

These swords are beautiful, with an austere perfection of line and proportion—surely the very essence of beauty—comparable with splendid and majestic pottery. A good sword has affinities with, let us say, the work of Chinese potters of the Sung dynasty— affinities whose impact is sharpened by the disparity in their *raison d'être*.

The "Knightly" sword is derived, via the swords of the Viking and Migration periods, from the long iron swords of the pre-historic Celts. These weapons of the first four centuries B.C., numbers of which have been found in various parts of Europe, have broad, flat blades with two cutting edges running nearly parallel to each other and ending in spatulate or rounded points. Most of the Continental ones have an average length of about 30″ from the point to the shoulders of the blade and about 6″ or 7″ from the shoulders to the top of the hilt. They are generally about 2″ wide at the hilt and taper to about $1\frac{1}{2}$″ at the point. It should be noted however that nearly all examples of Celtic swords found in the British Isles tend to be considerably smaller and of poor

[2] Egerton Castle, *Schools and Masters of Fence*, 1898.

quality, but the Continental ones are splendidly made. Most of them have a broad shallow fuller running the blade's length, while some of the finest have a double fuller.

These swords were used by Celtic and Teutonic barbarians throughout the Roman period. The cavalry auxiliaries of Rome, themselves generally Gaulish or German, were armed with the long sword (Spatha) in contrast to the short stabbing weapon (Gladius) of the legionary; many of these swords were unlike the barbarian ones, having narrow, pointed blades with a stiff, flat four or eight sided section very like a sword type of the 14th and 15th centuries A.D. A few of these Roman cavalry swords have been found in the Danish bog deposits, particularly at Vimose, alongside the commoner broadswords of the old Celtic and Teutonic types which by the 3rd century A.D. had been adopted in Scandinavia and the north, though in this period they tended to be of slighter proportions than their predecessors.

Towards the end of the Migration period broader and heavier blades predominated, and at some time about 900, during the Viking period, a new type of blade came into use, better balanced and more graceful in form. These blades were of the same proportions as some of the old Celtic ones, 30″ long from hilt to point and about 2″ wide at the hilt; they taper more sharply than their immediate predecessors and their point of balance is nearer to the hilt, so one can wield them with greater agility and speed. From this last type of blade, with the development of which the well-known bladesmith's firm of Ulfberht has been tentatively associated,[3] sprang the sword of the later Middle Ages.

The Nordic precursors of the knightly weapon have been analysed definitively in the classifications of Behmer[4] and Petersen,[5] while more recently the whole mystique of the Nordic sword has been dealt with very completely by Hilda Davidson, bringing the archaeological material of Behmer and Petersen and of later scholars into context with the art and literature of the first millennium of our era.[6] Therefore I shall only introduce these weapons where it is necessary to preserve continuity or explain evolution

[3] Jankuhn, H., *Ein Ulfberht-Schwert aus der Elbe bei Hamburg*, Festschrift f. Gustav Schwantes, Neuminster, 1951, pp. 212f.

[4] Behmer, Elis, *Das Zweischneidige Schwert der Deutschen Völkerwanderungszeit*, Stockholm, 1939.

[5] Petersen, Jan, *De Norske Vikingesverd*, 1919.

[6] Davidson, H. R. Ellis, *The Sword in Anglo-Saxon England*, Oxford, 1962.

in developing an analytical survey in which a typology may be worked out for the knightly sword, starting at the point where Petersen and Davidson left off, at the end of the Viking period.[7]

In most of the major museums of Europe, and in many small provincial ones too, a few swords will be found of the period between 1000 and 1500. Most of them will have been dug out of fields and ditches or found in the beds of rivers. Hardly any have been found in company with dateable objects, and most of them have knocked about in private collections for a generation or two before coming to rest in a museum, so that all knowledge of their find-place has been lost; indeed, too often a spurious tale of provenance has been acquired instead. There are so many of these that one hesitates to believe in the provenance of anything without documentation which is not suspect.

Though it has been possible to classify the European sword into clearly defined types and sub-types, it is not possible with the knowledge and material at present available to lay down any precise definitions of date or place. It will perhaps not be amiss in these introductory remarks to enlarge somewhat on that statement. To begin with, what do we mean when we seek a date for an object like a sword? Do we mean the approximate year in which it might have been made, or first acquired by an owner, or the period during which it might have been in use? We may suppose, for example, that a sword blade made in 1250 may not have been supplied to a hilt-maker and fitted up for several years. So it may not have become a weapon until 1254. Let us suppose that at that date it became the property of a young knight, who carried it until his death in 1300. Then the effigy upon his tomb might have been made in 1303, showing him armed with a sword at his side. The 20th century antiquarian would be justified in supposing that this effigy shows the harness and equipment of a fashionable knight of 1300; but what evidence is there that this is so? A knight, even a wealthy one, might not fit himself out with a complete new equipment every few years to follow the trend of

[7] A typology of the medieval two-edged sword has been produced (Hoffmeyer, Ada Bruhn, *Middelalderens Tvaeeggede Sverd*, Copenhagen, 1954) based upon pommel and cross styles, and only covering limited material. It does however contain an invaluable (though of necessity incomplete) catalogue of surviving specimens, and a great many photographs, in most cases only showing part of the sword. This work is of the very greatest value to the student.

fashion. More likely, individual items would be replaced as they wore out. His shield, for instance. Any man-at-arms who did a normal amount of fighting would undoubtedly wear out many shields in a lifetime, but his helmet and sword might last him out, and his body-armour would be repairable in its individual pieces and expensive to replace in toto. So, the sword shown at the side of this hypothetical effigy could be similar to the knight's own sword, carried throughout his life and at his burial coffined with his body or hung over his tomb. So it might represent a sword of 1258, not of 1300. Further bedevilment of the question arises when we remember that most fighting men had more than one sword, nor can the question possibly be resolved unless we know whether the effigies on knightly tombs show them armed in the fashion of their lifetimes, or in the fashion of the time of the tombs' making, maybe a decade or two before or after the knight's death. It seems probable that some tombs do indeed show arms contemporary with the lifetime of their occupant, while others show arms fashionable only after his demise. But which? The monument in gilded latten of the Black Prince in Canterbury Cathedral is an example of the former. It is now recognised that the helm, and the gauntlets of gilt copper, which hung above this tomb are actual habiliments of war, which the Prince could have used. These are so exactly reproduced by the helm and gauntlets on the effigy that it is clear that all the rest of the armour it shows must be contemporary with the Prince's lifetime.

The exact opposite is the case with the equally splendid monument of Richard Beauchamp, Earl of Warwick, in St. Mary's Church, Warwick. This great magnate died in 1432, but the effigy was not fashioned until twenty years later: the bill for its making still exists: "W. Austen, citizen and founder of London, covenants to cast and make an image of a man armed, of fine latten, garnished with certain ornaments, viz. with a sword and dagger, with a Garter, with a helm and crest under his head and at his feet a bear muzzled and a griffin perfectly made of finest latten, according to patterns." Were these patterns (models for the armour, sword, helm, etc.) supplied from the Earl's own equipment, or were they supplied by armourers? If the Earl's own armour was used, it would probably be his latest. If it was borrowed, might not the armourer (or whoever else William Austen got his model from) lend an old one? So many questions, so many possible answers. In this particular case it seems that whatever the source of the "patterns", the armour at least is the best and most up-to-date available in the 1450's, for it corresponds closely to Milanese armours known to be of this date. But what of the numerous freestone and alabaster monuments of lesser men, ordinary knights and country squires? There are two bills and accounts surviving for effigies of this kind during the first half of the 15th century, where phrases akin to "according to patterns" appear, making it clear enough that the executors of the deceased expected the effigy to be shown in correct armour, but no evidence has appeared as yet to show whether this was to be his own armour, or simply armour as worn at the time of the fashioning of the tomb.

In these two magnificent monuments (which by their quality are only comparable with each other) we have the two opposites. The Black Prince's figure gives us a terminus post quem, for his arms are clearly those of his lifetime; the Earl's gives us a terminus ante quem, for *his* are of the latest fashion in a period twenty years after his death. With all the multitude of monuments in Europe we can only take the middle way, to assume that the armour and weapons they show in such clear detail may be of styles in use either before or after the lifetime of the warrior lying beneath them; in attempting a date we have to allow latitude of a couple of decades either way.

So in trying to date a sword or a sword-type, it is perhaps more practical to look for a period during which it could have been in use, though this might cover a span of time too long to be of value. In the Norse literature there is much evidence for swords being continuously in use for several generations, or being used by one man for a lifetime, then being stored for another generation to be given to a descendant for a further lifetime of use.[8] Here a span of well over a century may be involved. The evidence for similarly long lifetimes of swords in the later Middle Ages is not so plentiful or so precise, but there is too much to be disregarded. Some compromise must be sought, areas of probability into which swords of specific types and fashions may be fitted, suggesting as nearly as possible a terminus ante quem. In some cases a terminus post quem may be provided by individual examples, such as swords from the tombs of princes, but this leaves the

[8] See, e.g,, Davidson, op. cit. pp. 118–121.

problem of the weapon's real date (by which we may assume its date of birth, as it were) unresolved.

There are a number of factors which provide dating evidence, but few can do more than suggest a position within a half-century. Evidence of fashion, as shown by varying and developing styles of hilt, becomes more useful towards the end of the period, but is quite valueless at the beginning; different techniques of inlay in blade inscriptions and the styles of the inscriptions themselves are invaluable for classification but need to be handled with caution in dating. The presence of identifiable heraldic bearings can give a tolerably firm date—in one well-known example to within two years—but this only gives the date at which the arms were applied to the weapon. It by no means follows that the date of the arms is the date of the sword's making, but of its purchase or presentation. Still less do they give a terminating date, unless they were found in a tomb.

The mounts of scabbards are generally taken to be reliable evidence of date. So they are, but for the scabbard, not for the sword. Scabbards must have been replaced fairly often, particularly in the Middle Ages when they were continually worn in the open air, exposed to heat and wet as well as ordinary wear and tear. A well-loved sword might have had several scabbards during its working life, and each new scabbard's mounts would reflect the fashion of the time at which it was made. So too it must have been with grips. These must have been replaced sometimes, and would similarly show fashion changes.

So, then, sword forms may be grouped and classified, but only vaguely dated. They fall clearly into two groups, divided by a radical change of form brought about by an equally drastic change in the defensive armour to which they were opposed. This change took place roughly between 1275 and 1350, a transitional period of three-quarters of a century during which some specific transitional types appeared. It may be safe to say that a blade of one of the types in Group 1 (blades which were made to oppose armour of mail) should date before 1300, and one in Group 2 (made to oppose armour of plate) should date after 1350; but since the period of the Group 1 blades extends from about 1000 to 1300, and of Group 2 blades from 1350 to 1550, only vague and imprecise dating can be obtained. This is further complicated by the fact that blades of some of the types in Group 1 became popular again after 1450. The transitional types, made to be effective against armour either of mail or of plate, or a mixture of the two, are the only ones which with reasonable assurance can be dated within the span of half a century.

Luckily we are not confined to the study of purely archaeological evidence for dating our sword-types. The countless medieval works of art which show swords and armour—indeed every kind of weapon and all forms of military equipment—are of the first importance, and the archaeologist is fortunate that the medieval artist was a most literal-minded individual and no archaeologist himself; he drew or sculpted what he saw, neither more nor less, his work unspoiled by distortions and affectations masquerading under the name of Art. There were of course some medieval artists whose work is bad, but this can be overlooked as there is so much which is good. Much of this work is dateable to within a year or two, or at most a decade or two. The question which arises in assessing its value in dating the various objects illustrated is the same as the one affecting tomb effigies. The work itself shows that the artist was either himself acquainted with the militaria he illustrated, or that he drew from models. Were these models necessarily the most up-to-date available? A 13th century painter, illustrating a manuscript with scenes from the wars of Saul and David, would be likely to draw from equipment in general use at the time he was doing the work, though we cannot reject the possibility that he might have been soldiering in his youth and drew what he remembered. One asset in all these unhelpful possibilities is that the artists in every period of the Middle Ages, in most parts of Europe, show remarkable consistency in their work. Choose any period, and it will be found that tomb effigies, decorative figure sculpture and manuscript paintings all show the same kind of armour and arms with only minor variations. If we take the reasonable assumption that what was painted or carved was what was currently in use, we can align our archaeological material and facts with it and so arrive at reasonable datings in half or quarter centuries.

This method has been used in the following classifications, but it must be accepted that new finds or hitherto unknown (or unnoticed) documents may affect the conclusions arrived at.

The problems which beset any attempt to assign specific regions of origin for our sword-types are easier to deal with, for they are insuperable. It just cannot be done. Even in the Viking and Migration periods it has only been possible to suggest tentatively that certain clearly-defined types (types of hilt and styles of decoration, be it understood—blades were hardly considered by Petersen and Behmer) come from one region or another. This is based upon find-distribution and decorative style. But in those times, much roving and raiding was done by bands of warriors and by individuals; they may have left their weapons in their distant wanderings or died in far-away places, or they may have been despoiled of them or (in some cases) have parted with them in exchange for the weapons of other warriors. Thus, a sword of a more or less specific Norwegian type may be found in a grave in Bulgaria, or a Frankish type in Jugoslavia[9], but this is no indication that one was a Bulgarian sword and the other a Dalmatian. In the High Middle Ages we do not even have these regional classifications to help us. Now and then an oddly shaped or decorated hilt may appear,[10] but in the main swords show remarkable uniformity within the framework of types from Finland to Sicily and from the 11th century to the 16th. In the swords of the 15th century there do seem to have been vague fashions which lead one into the temptation of saying that a sword may be of Italian or of German style; this is based largely on the frequency with which one set of styles or the other appears in Italian or German paintings. There is however one type which seems to have been of definite Scandinavian origin, most of its examples dating between perhaps 1440 and 1480.[11]

Swords were very distributable things during the Age of Chivalry. Consider some of the ways in which an Englishman might acquire a sword: he might buy it in his nearest town, or at a fair from a traveller for one of the great weapon-making firms of Milan or Passau, Augsburg or Cologne or Bordeaux. Wherever he bought it, the blade would certainly have been made in one or other of these places, though the hilt might have

[9] For instance, there is a group of swords of Petersen's Type K found in graves in Jugoslavia at Biskupija near Knin, and Koljani. *Zeitschrift fur Historische Waffen- und Kostum-Kunde*. (This periodical will hereafter be referred to as Z.H.W.K.) IV, 4, p. 99.

[10] Such as a Scandinavian sword of the 12th century, illustrated in Laking, Sir G. F., *A Record of European Armour and Arms*, London, 1920, vol. I, p. 102, fig. 124; and a similar one in the National Museum at Copenhagen.

[11] Type XVIIIe, see Chapter II, p. 72.

been made in Paris or London—or Salisbury or Chester, Norwich or Gloucester. Or he might have been given it by his feudal superior who might have been a baron of Normandy who had won the sword in personal combat with a Spanish knight who had got the sword in Seville. Or he might have got it on a battlefield in Aquitaine or at a tournament in Saxony. Whomsoever *he* had overcome to win it might have had it from a place remote from his own land. Or, again, he may have been given it by a relative, a family treasure honourably borne half a century before and won in Sicily.

When our hypothetical English knight parted with this imaginary weapon, ultimately to be found by the 20th century archaeologist, he may have died in possession of it and had it placed in his tomb. Or he may have dropped it or lost it while crossing a river in Brittany; or *he* may have been overcome at a jousting in Provence by a knight from Prussia, who might have taken it home and had it hung over *his* tomb; or he might have bestowed it upon a brother-in-arms in Outremer—there is literally no end to the vicissitudes which any excavated sword in any provincial museum may have suffered before its burial.

So I firmly adhere to the archaeological heresy that knowledge of the find-place of any sword is utterly valueless in dating or placing it. Even if this find-place is inside an unbroken tomb upon an identifiable body, it only gives its latest date, no reliable place of origin. Finds in fields and rivers are useless, and even finds on the known sites of battles may be suspect. On the field of Bosworth a sword was found in the 18th century, and for some time[12] was believed to have been lost in the battle of 1485; but it is a "dish-hilt" rapier of *c.* 1640. In the River Witham near Lincoln a group of swords were recovered in 1788 near the site of Stephen's battle of 1141; but one sword was of the Iron Age, six dated between 1100 and 1350, and one was a broken backsword blade of about 1660. Only one could, by its style, have been used in the battle of 1141.

In the following typologies certain swords found on battlefields have been used as fixed dating-points, but this is really a measure taken in desperation, as it were, for sheer lack of anything better. The number of medieval swords whose actual date can be determined has been growing steadily in recent years, but

[12] Hutton, W., *Bosworth Field*, London, 1813, fig. 4.

there are still lamentably few which can be used confidently as "fixed points" to support typological analysis.

The material selected here for illustration tries to do two things: one, to present to the reader the finest available specimens of the various types—not the richest or the most elaborate, but the best-preserved of typical examples; and two, to illustrate as far as possible weapons which have not been published previously, and which are not readily available to the student. There are of course exceptions; swords from the Armouries of the Tower of London, and from the Wallace Collection in London, in the Musée de l'Armée in Paris and the Kunsthistorisches Museum in Vienna have to be included because of their importance to the typology; but with them appear some remarkably fine swords from private collections, small provincial museums and inaccessible Cathedral treasuries.

The method of numbering the typologies of complete swords, of pommels and of cross-guards has been worked out in such a way that any sword can be described adequately and clearly by a formula. For the complete sword-types, Roman numerals have been used; for pommels, letters; and for cross-guards, arabic numerals. So a sword (as in fig. 1) could be described as: XII, B1, 1, which clearly defines first the form of the whole sword, second the type of pommel, and lastly the style of the cross-guard.

The sword typologies worked out by Behmer and Petersen were based mainly upon styles of hilt, and hilt and scabbard-mount ornamentation, taking little or no account of the shape of blades, but this will not do for the swords of the Age of Chivalry, for the form of their blades gives the essential key to any classification. In fact, to attempt to classify these later weapons on hilt-forms alone is impossible; the only way to do it seems to be to base a typology on *proportion*, the proportions of the whole sword, entirely disregarding the kind of pommel or cross-guard it may have. In a paper published in 1950, I made a serious error in stating that the exact opposite was the case, following the lead of earlier authorities.[13] The years of further study seem to show that

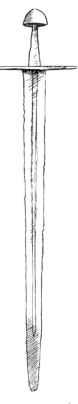

Fig. 1. Sword,
Type XII,
c. 1150.
Historisches
Museum, Berne.

[13] Oakeshott, R. Ewart, "A Fifteenth Century 'Royal' Sword", The Connoisseur, June, 1950. ". . . It is possible to classify individually these three elements (i.e. blade, pommel and cross) of a medieval sword, and often by means of this classification to date them within a decade or so; but clearly there must be some overlapping of date-able styles when the three are assembled in one weapon. So we may arrive at a more just assessment of a sword's date if we treat these elements separately when making comparisons."

though pommels and cross-guards, in their infinite variety, may themselves be classified, the sword itself must depend upon its blade-form and the relative proportions of its parts, for many of the pommel-types were in use throughout the whole period, and it seems that it must have been very largely a matter of personal taste which determined the type of pommel a sword had. This is even more the case when it comes to the cross-guard—the "Quillons" as this feature is often but incorrectly called. This is a late term; there is no evidence to show that it was ever used before the end of the 16th century; before that, and particularly during the later Middle Ages, this part of a sword hilt was invariably called the cross if it was specified at all. During the Migration and Viking periods there was little variation in the actual shape of this cross, such differences as there were being more a matter of decoration than of actual form. After about 1120, however, there began to be a great deal of variety, not ornamental at all. There are infinite diversities in the shape, length, weight and bulk of crosses—diversities which again were probably a result of personal fancy or the dictates of fashion, for they are in no way regional; and since nearly all the styles appear indiscriminately throughout the whole of the period, they are quite useless for dating purposes. However, allowing for much variation of detail, they do fall into definite groups and so may be classified.

So the following typologies are based purely and simply upon an aesthetic standard, form and proportion being the only criteria. This may seem to be a serious archaeological heresy; the only excuse I can offer for it is that it works.

Some scholars, in writing of swords, have elected to describe them as if they were viewed in a position with the hilt downward and the point up.[14] Others (the great majority) take the opposite view, and see the sword with its hilt uppermost. This I have done, partly because it seems natural, but principally because it is the way the sword is described clearly in the Norse literature. Here the words "upper hilt" and "lower hilt" are often used in speaking of the pommel and its cross-guard respectively. Then again, where decoration is applied in the form of lettered inscriptions to the crosses of knightly swords, these are always so placed that they can

[14] e.g. the Catalogue of the Arms and Armour in the Wallace Collection in London; Wallace Collection Catalogues. European Arms and Armour. Mann, Sir James, K.C.V.O., F.B.A., Hon. V-P.S.A. 1962.

be read only if the hilt is held upwards. Similarly arms applied to the pommel are upside-down when the sword is held with its point up, and can only be seen properly when the sword is in its correct position, i.e. with the point down. Similarly when marks of a pictographic nature are applied singly (as maker's marks) to the blade—helms, shields, swords and daggers; in one example in Copenhagen a bull's head—they are the right way up only if the sword is point downward.

The exception to these facts is of course to be found in swords of state and ceremony—"bearing swords" as they were called in medieval times. Here the reverse is always the case, for they had only to be seen when held point upwards. Such weapons have probably been the cause of the confusion.

A chapter has been included to deal with the perishable fittings which were essential to turn the fundamental ironwork of a sword into a usable weapon—the grip and the scabbard. Within the rather rigid limitations of its practical form, the grip varied a good deal. There were changes in its outline and in the material with which it was covered, all very clearly shown in works of art and in a good many cases in surviving examples. It should how-ever always be borne in mind that a surviving sword with an obviously ancient grip still in place may have in its time had several, which wore out or were damaged, and replaced. In this way an obviously 15th century sword may survive with an obviously "original" 16th century grip.

In dealing with scabbards, it is the mounts only which can be classified. The actual scabbard itself, its materials and method of construction, varied not at all (or hardly at all) from the Bronze Age until the 17th century.

The typology of swords may seem to have serious omissions, but these are deliberate. It is for the straight, two-edged, cross-hilted sword of the kind which is generally (and very rightly, if somewhat romantically) called "Knightly". Curved swords are a class on their own, needing their own separate typological analysis. Two-hand swords, before about 1520, are only very big examples of some of the ordinary types, and the short Italianate sword, of which the Cinquedea is the best-known form, are extremely hybrid; and since their use seems to have been mainly after the 16th century, they belong to the Renaissance rather than to the Age of Chivalry.

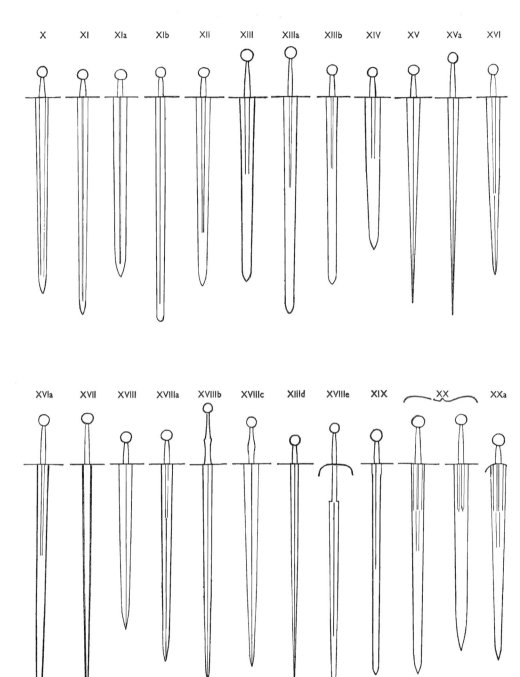

X   XI   XIa   XIb   XII   XIII   XIIIa   XIIIb   XIV   XV   XVa   XVI

XVIa   XVII   XVIII   XVIIIa   XVIIIb   XVIIIc   XIIId   XVIIIe   XIX   XX   XXa

CHAPTER ONE

Swords of Group I (1050–1350)

THIS typology begins, quite deliberately, with Type X (Ten). This is because the "Knightly" sword emerges imperceptibly from the later Viking types which preceded it. The careful and most thorough analysis of Viking sword-types made in 1919 by Dr. Jan Petersen has become the standard typology for swords of this period, in use all over Europe, but in 1927 a condensed and simplified version of it was presented by Dr. R. E. M. (now Sir Mortimer) Wheeler,[1] which ever since has been the classification to which English students turn. It begins with Type I, and goes on to Type VII. To this I have added two types, Nos. VIII and IX which bridge the never clearly defined transition from the Viking sword to the Knightly one. Thus the first of the later medieval types becomes Type X.

Elis Behmer's classification of the swords of the Migration period comprises 9 types and sub-types, most comprehensively covering the swords of this period (*c.* 250–*c.* 700), and for convenience a simplified

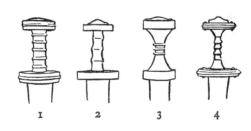

Fig. 2. *Behmer's typology.*

version of it has been worked out, similar to Wheeler's simplification of Petersen, which, to avoid confusion with the twenty Viking and medieval types, has been numbered 1 to 4 in Arabic numerals.[2] Diagrams of these two simplified typologies are given in figs. 2 and 3.

[1] Wheeler, R. E. M., *London and the Vikings* (London Museum Catalogue), 1927.
[2] Oakeshott, R. Ewart, *The Archaeology of Weapons*, Lutterworth Press, 1960, chap. 7, fig. 41, p. 107.

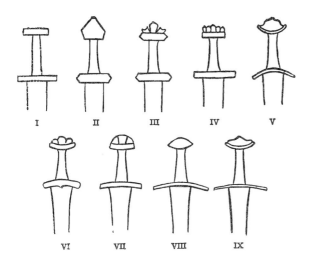

I   II   III   IV   V

VI   VII   VIII   IX

Fig. 3. Wheeler's typology.

The four basic types of Migration period swords are hilt types. They were all fitted with simple two-edged blades which varied a good deal in size but not much in shape. There was however one distinction; some blades were comparatively slender and quite acutely pointed, while the majority were broad, with almost parallel edges and spatulate points. The Norse peoples themselves made a distinction, for they had four words for a sword; two of them, *svaerd* and *maekir*, seem to be applied to these two kinds of blade;[3] svaerd, the more usual term, seems to apply to the broad slashing blade, while maekir denotes the slender pointed type. Many blades have survived, but there are far more hilts because they were so often made of imperishable gold or bronze. They are nearly all of rich material and are often of dazzling workmanship, even the less magnificent comparable in beauty with goldsmith's work of the Renaissance, and often exceeding it in craftsmanship. These were the swords of chieftains in a period when only the great and powerful bore this weapon.

During the following age of the Vikings swords were much more widely used, and consequently many were hilted with great simplicity in plain iron, or even bone or wood. Even so, a high proportion are richly bedight, though very few can compare with the earlier ones in this respect. Here again the type-variation is to be found in the hilts, in their form and adornment, not in the blades. These of course vary considerably in size and weight, for so did the men who used them, but their form was pretty constant. Some, like their immediate predecessors, had wide and shallow fullers, some had deeper, narrower ones while others had double[4] or treble ones[5]—and a few had none. Otherwise all conformed to

---

[3] Shetelig, H., *Scandinavian Archaeology*, and Oakeshott, op. cit., Chap. 9, p. 150.

[4] Double fullers were also common in swords of the la Tène culture.

[5] e.g. a sword in the possession of Dr. Richard Williams, of Type X.

the same basic pattern, well exemplified by a splendid example from the Thames at Shifford, near Reading.[6] On the strength of find-distribution and decorative style, Wheeler has suggested[7] that these seven hilt varieties may have been typical of certain regions of usage and manufacture: I and II, Norway; III, north-west Germany and southern Scandinavia; IV, universal all over Europe; V, Anglo-Saxon England; VI,

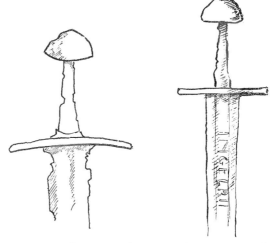

Fig. 4. *Brazil-nut pommel. from a grave at Sandeherred, Norway, c. 950. Type VIII (Petersen's Type X).*

Fig. 5. *Tea-Cosy pommel. Sword found in the River Isac. Nantes, c. 950. Type VIIIa (Petersen's Type X).*

Denmark, and VII, a late type used by the Danes and distributed widely along the western European seaboard.

Types VIII and IX, which Wheeler omitted since in 1927 they were generally supposed to be of post-Viking date, provide the link between the two periods. In fact specimens of both types have been found in Viking graves of the 10th century,[8] but so many have come out of rivers—admittedly Viking-infested during the 10th and 11th centuries—and from far afield in Central Europe where Viking raids were rare or unheard of, that it may be reasonable to classify them as of Germanic, but Christian, origin. Examples of the *hilt* type, too, seem to be datable up to the 13th century and may be found on swords of Type X and XI, even on XII and XIII.

These two types, VIII and IX, are distinguished like their predecessors by their hilt-forms, for most are fitted with ordinary Viking blades. They represent swords which did not have the rather elaborate pommels of the more typical Viking weapons. VIII can be divided into two types, VIII and VIIIa. The former is furnished with a pommel shaped like a Brazil nut (fig. 4 and plate 1C) while the latter's pommel is rather similar but with a straight

[6] Reading Museum, also one from the Witham, British Museum (plate 1A).

[7] Wheeler, *London and the Vikings*, op. cit., p. 30–36.

[8] One of Type VIII in a grave at Sandeherred, Norway (Petersen, *De Norske Vikingesverd*, p. 166, fig. 129), and one of Type IX in a grave at Flemma, in Tingvoll, Norway. Bruhn Hoffmeyer, plate Ve, and Petersen, "Gravfunnene pa Flemma i Tingvoll", Arsskrift for Nordmor Historielag, 1925, p. 36ff.

lower edge (fig. 5). Once called "of mushroom form", I would suggest that it is more realistic to call it "of tea-cosy form",[9] for it is comparatively flat in plan like an empty tea-cosy, while the plumper varieties are like the same object with a teapot inside. The Brazil-nut forms (there are many varieties, fully discussed in chapter III below) have mostly been found in north-eastern, central and eastern Europe, while the Tea-Cosy ones have nearly all come from western Europe, often in coastal areas settled by the Danes in the 9th and 10th centuries—areas roughly corresponding to the old Carolingian regions of Austrasia and Neustria.

Fig. 6. *Cocked-hat pommel, from a grave at Flemma, Norway, c. 1000. Type IX (Petersen's Type Y).*

Type IX has a pommel like a cocked hat[10] (fig. 6), and is far more rare than the other two. In a more developed form it was much used during the 12th and 13th centuries, particularly in Germany. This too is fully discussed in chapter III.

These hilt types VIII and IX are often to be found on swords of Type X, and confusion is added to complication because our Types VIII and IX are in fact Petersen's Types X and Y.[11] I have tried to work out some simple way of clearly differentiating my own Type X (ten) from Petersen's Type X, but nothing can really be done. Perhaps the crossing, as it were, of the two typologies at this point, at a sword-type common to both, may be regarded as a pivot around which the two may swing in harmony.

TYPE X CHARACTERISTICS

A broad, flat *blade* of medium length (average 31″) with a fuller running the entire length and fading out an inch or so from the point, which is sometimes acute but more often rounded. This fuller is generally very wide and shallow, but in some cases may be narrower (about $\frac{1}{3}$ of the blade's width) and more clearly defined; a short *grip*, of the same average length ($3\frac{3}{4}$″) as the Viking

Type X

[9] Oakeshott, R. Ewart, Journal of the British Archaeological Association, June, 1951, Vol. XIV, "Some Medieval Sword-pommels".

[10] Petersen, *De Norske Vikingesverd*, op. cit., p. 167ff., figs. 130, 131, 132; and Bruhn Hoffmeyer, op. cit., vol. II, plate V.

[11] ibid.

swords. The *tang* is usually very flat and broad, tapering sharply towards the pommel. The *cross* is narrower and longer than the more usual Viking kind—though the Vikings used it, calling it "Gaddhjalt" (spike-hilt) because of its spike-like shape. Generally of square section, about 7″ to 8″ long, tapering towards the tips. In rare cases curved. The *pommel* is commonly of one of the Brazil-nut forms, but may be of disc form.

General Remarks

This type may too easily be confused with Type VIII. Many swords of the two types—compare plates 1C and 2C—look identical in shape. In such cases, the only possible way out is to make use of any internal evidence the specimen itself may afford, such as inlaid marks and inscriptions in the blade. Many of these swords—of both types—are from the INGELRIÍ workshops, while others bear similar smith-names inlaid in big iron letters. If on the reverse of such blades we find what may be called a Christian inscription (for instance INNOMINEDOMINI or a garbled version of it)[12] or a pattern of non-pagan character inlaid in a different metal, such as latten or tin (or silver), then the sword would be of Type X. Good examples of both can be seen on plates 1 and 2. 1C is a sword in my own collection, with the name Ingelrií on one side and a pattern (fig. 7) similarly inlaid on the other, which is characteristic of the Viking-age patterns so familiar upon the ULF-BERHT swords. 2C is a sword in the Museum of Ethnology and Archaeology at Cambridge. On one side it has the name CON-STAININUS and on the other the words INNOMINEDNI—both in big iron letters. 1C, therefore, is of Type VIII, while 2C is of Type X. The hilts of the two appear to be identical, but the pommel of 1C is rather plump, whereas that of 2C is quite flat. Only in elevation do they look identical.

Fig. 7. *Inlays on a sword-blade, c. 950. Type VIII.* (*plate 1C*)

Many of the Type X swords

[12] For instance, an Ingelrii sword in the Zweizerisches Landesmuseum in Zurich (plate 2A and fig. 127) has the smith-name on one side of the blade, and the words "Homodei" in smaller iron letters on the other. Inv. No. 16203, Bruhn Hoffmeyer, plate IXa and p. 9, No. 26; and Wegeli, R., *Inschriften auf Mittelalterliche Schwertklingen*, Z.H.W.K., 1903, fig. 7.

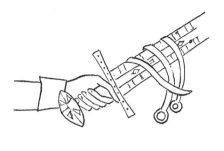

Fig. 8. Figure from "The Gospels of Otto III". Bamberg. Made at Reichenau between 983–991.

Fig. 9. From a Sacramentary made in Regensburg between 1002–1024.

have very wide Brazil-nut pommels (plate 2A); this is a clear distinction from Type VIII. Others (plate 2B) have a disc pommel. Here again there need be no confusion. It is only where a sword has a small Brazil-nut pommel and spike cross and an uninscribed blade that it may equally well be of either type.

There is a certain amount of variety in the shape of these blades, though most of them are identical. Some have very sharp points, some very blunt ones (though we may assume these to be corroded and broken off), though the majority have a subtly rounded point which looks as if it would be of little use in thrusting. Plate 2 gives examples of all three kinds of point, and the variations in the form of the fuller.

The type is adequately represented in art, though hardly at all in sculpture. This lack however is amply compensated by the frequency with which it appears in manuscript illustrations. The variety with the wide Brazil-nut pommel seems to have been very popular with German illuminators of the Ottonian period (c. 950–1050)[13] (figs. 8 and 9) and appears again on decorated metalwork about 1100 (figs. 10 and 11).[14]

[13] E. G. Munich, Staatsbibliothek Cod. Lat. 4453, "Gospels of Otto III" between 983 and 991; many swords of Type VIIIA are also shown here, and one of Petersen's Type N (not included specifically in Wheeler's typology, but actually a version of Type VII); also Cod. Lat. 4456, a Sacramentary from the Cathedral Treasury at Bamberg, made for the Emperor Henry II between 1002 and 1024. A sword of Petersen's Type K—Wheeler's Type IV—appears in this MS; for many facsimiles from these and other MSS of the Ottonian period see Adolf Goldschmidt, *Die Deutsche Buchmalerei*, vol II, 1928.

Fig. 10. St. Simplicius. From an engraved copper-gilt altar, c. 1100. Victoria and Albert Museum.

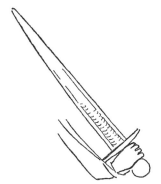

Fig. 11. From an engraved altar at Stavelot, c. 1120.

TYPE XI CHARACTERISTICS

A long, narrow *blade*, sharply contrasting with the broad, short blades of Type X, the edges running parallel for about $\frac{2}{3}$ of the blade's length, then tapering in subtle curves to an adequate point. The fuller is narrow, often very shallow and poorly defined, and runs $\frac{4}{5}$ of the blade's length, sometimes (in later examples) beginning in the tang within the hilt. The *cross* in most surviving examples tends to be straight and of rectangular section, while the majority of *pommels* are of the various Brazil-nut forms, though a good many have disc pommels. A few have thick disc pommels with strongly bevelled edges (Type H—see chapter III). The *tang* is short, generally with parallel sides, and not so flat as in the Type X swords.

General Remarks

This type has generally been held to belong to the period *c.* 1120–*c.* 1200–1220, but recent research has given a much earlier

Type XI

[14] There are many portable altars ("Tragaltar") of engraved copper-gilt, Rhenish work mostly made between 1100 and 1150, upon which are many scenes of martyrdoms and sword-bearing saints (i.e. St. George, St. Michael, St. Paul, St. Simplicius, St. Theodore, St. Catherine) whereon swords of Type X are shown. One of these, showing St. Simplicius, is in the Victoria and Albert Museum in London (fig. 10). The series is well covered by A. Falke, *Deutsche Schmelzarbeiten des Mittelalters*, 1904. Fig. 11, from a Tragaltar at Stavelot, the work of Godefroid de Claire, shows a sword very similar to the sword in the Musée de l'Armée in Paris, plate 2B. A sculptured figure showing a hilt with one of the wide Brazil-nut pommels is on a capital in the church of St. Nectaire in Southern France. This shows one of the guards at the sepulchre. Another capital showing the same subject—almost certainly by the same hand—in the church at Mozac has a sword with a hilt of Type VIIIa. These sculptures are dated at about 1140, and suggest that the VIIIa pommels were still used as late as this.

possible date. A sword of this type (plate 4A) recently examined[15] has been found to have runes engraved on the tang and inlaid in white metal in the blade. The runes on the tang are of a distinctively Anglo-Saxon character,[16] and of 10th century date at the latest—runes were little used by the Anglo-Saxons after about 900.[17] The well-formed Brazil-nut pommel and the long, almost imperceptibly curved cross are both of a form hitherto held to be of a date no earlier than *c.* 1100,[18] but there is actually plenty of evidence that they were in use, particularly in England, during the 10th century.[19] Several English manuscripts,[20] datable within that century, show long, slender swords (fig. 12) with hilts much akin to this example; in some cases the cross is extremely long, and very sharply curved. There is a pommel, too, in the British Museum,[21] found at Ingleton in Yorkshire with a mount of silver gilt nielloed and decorated in a typically English style of *c.* 900 which is—or was, for the iron part is much corroded—very similar indeed in shape to the pommel on the sword in question, and to those in the manuscripts referred to.

Thus it would appear that the type was in use at least as early as *c.* 1000.

Another sword of this type which may be considered to some extent datable is the magnificent weapon in the Schatzkammer in Vienna, formerly used as a ceremonial sword at the coronations of Emperors and known as the Sword of St. Maurice. It has always been considered that this could be dated firmly at 1198–1215, for upon the pommel of gilded iron (formerly said to be of silver) are engraved arms which seemed to indicate the treaty made in 1208 between the Emperor Otto IV and John of England; on one side are the arms of the Empire, and on the other a shield of a demi-eagle impaling three leopards.[22] Hence the whole

---

[15] Sotheby's, April 28th, 1961, Lot 131, Author's collection.

[16] This information has been imparted by Dr. H. R. E. Davidson.

[17] ibid., and Dr. H. R. E. Davidson, *The Sword in Anglo-Saxon England*, Oxford, 1960.

[18] i.e. Laking, Sir G. F., *A Record of European Armour and Arms*, 1920, vol. I. London Museum Catalogue, No. 7 (Medieval Catalogue).

[19] Davidson, op. cit.

[20] e.g. British Museum. Cott. MS. Nero CIV, & CVI.

[21] B.M. Quarterly, XV, 1941–50, p. 74.
Davidson, *The Sword in Anglo-Saxon England*, p. 69–70, fig. 46.

[22] Laking, op. cit., vol. I, chap. III, fig. 119, p. 97–98.

weapon was deemed to date between those years, but now that it has been worked upon further a different story has emerged. The arms were in fact those used personally by Otto IV, and have nothing to do with England. The blade (plate 5B) is enclosed in a very magnificent scabbard, decorated with gold panels showing repoussé figures of monarchs, with bands of enamel-work between each panel. The sheath itself is of olive-wood. Now, as we shall see later (chapter V) a sword's scabbard was made by using the blade as a mandril around which the long, very thin strips of wood were formed to a perfect fit; and upon these slats any covering, of leather or velvet or of gold or silver or whatever it may have been, was as closely fitted. Thus, every individual blade had its own scabbard, which no other blade would be likely to fit. Using these data, it can be said with assurance that the gold panels on the scabbard in question were made to fit the sheath that fitted the blade. A careful examination of the figures embossed upon the panels shows, stylistically, that they are of 11th century date; of this there is no question. And they were clearly made to fit over the sheath itself; there is no evidence (quite the contrary) to show that they might have been altered to fit the sheath, even allowing such a cheese-paring piece of economising to have been possible. So the sheath too must be of the 11th century, and so, *ipso facto*, must the blade. These figures on the sheath, incidentally, are put on it in such a position that to stand upright the sheathed sword must be held, in the manner of a "Bearing Sword" with the point upward. So it seems it was never made for a sword in ordinary use, worn at a knightly belt, for then the golden monarchs would have had to stand on their heads.

When we come to examine the little bands of enamel, done in tiny squares, white and blue and red, forming a diaper pattern, which separate the gold panels, we find that they are as characteristic of the early 13th century as the panels are of the 11th. The hilt too is of a kind previously regarded as typical of the same period (*c.* 1200), though it is very similar to the 10th century sword of Type XI described above (plate 4A), and may well be contemporary with the blade; but engraved upon the cross are the words *Cristus Vincit. Cristus Reinat. Cristus Inperat.* These words were used as the antiphon to the Coronation Anthem "Laudes Regiae" as well as a war-cry by the hosts of the 3rd Crusade, so it

Type XIa

may be inferred that on this sword they are of that, or a subsequent, date. So what emerges is that in the time of Otto IV (probably for his coronation), the scabbard was embellished with the enamel bands, and the hilt was engraved—the whole thing in fact was "done up" for Otto IV.[23] So now, instead of having a complete sword datable at about 1210, we have an 11th century blade fitted with clearly dated 13th century decoration; and as this weapon has hitherto been used as a dating-point to put blades of Type XI into the 13th century, we must now re-date the type.

Several of these swords, two with flat disc pommels,[24] two with thick ones with bevelled edges,[25] and one with a Brazil-nut pommel, are inscribed with the words GICELIN ME FECIT one side and INNOMINEDOMINI on the other, each inscription having a cross potent at either end, and all being inlaid with iron in the manner of the Ulfberht and Ingelrii swords. The only difference is that in these Type XI weapons the letters are very much smaller, and so appear to be neater. (They are not, really. Magnify them to the dimensions of the Ingelrii's, and they look remarkably similar.) This smallness and apparent neatness has caused scholars to assume that these inlays are a progression from the cruder, earlier ones, and are thus later in date.[26] Why? They *have* to be smaller, for they must be fitted into a very narrow fuller, not allowed to sprawl over a very wide one. In view of the rune-inscribed sword and the Vienna blade's date, it seems that these Gicelin swords, and others similarly inlaid, are probably datable between 1000 and 1100, not between 1150 and 1225. The "developed" disc pommel, also hitherto held to indicate a later date, does not in fact do so; for among many swords excavated in Finland in 1949–1950 from 11th century Viking graves have been these pommels—there was a sixth Gicelin sword too among the finds.[27]

Many swords of this type have finely-made inscriptions inlaid

[23] Weixlgärtner, A., Arpad. Jahrbuch der Kunsthistorische Sammlungen in Wien. N.F. I. 1926.

[24] Z.H.W.K. Band VII, 8. Schweitering, J., p. 211–14, fig. 1a; and Bruhn Hoffmeyer, pl. XII, d.g., pp. 15, 21, Copenhagen Nat. Mus. D. 7955 and Hamburg Mus. Gesch. M. 164.

[25] Z.H.W.K. ibid., p. 214, figs. 1g, 1c; and Bruhn Hoffmeyer, plate XII, h, i, p. 21. Berlin, Zeughaus.

[26] Z.H.W.K. Band III, R. Wegeli, op. cit.

[27] This information I had in the course of private correspondence with Dr. Jorma Leppaho of Helsinki, who found them.

with yellow metal (latten) or white (? silver or tin). This different style of inlay has also been taken as being of a later date[28] than the iron ones, though it is not easy to see why, for there are many saxes of the 9th and 10th centuries inlaid in fine, small letters of copper or latten,[29] which have been known for many decades. Now we have the small white metal inlays of the sword with the Anglo-Saxon runes (the reverse of that blade, incidentally, is inlaid for about 15″ in white metal with a small pattern of a herringbone character which seems by its appearance to be intended to simulate pattern-welding. Similar designs may be seen on sax-blades) as further evidence that such inlays were used in the 10th century.[30] One of these Type XI swords has an inscription in yellow metal reading SES BENEDICTAS on one side and +INOMINEDOM on the other. This sword—a very beautiful one— was found in a Suffolk ditch at Fornham, on the site of a battle fought in 1173 between Henry II and the Earl of Leicester. Here, maybe, is evidence of a Type XI sword being in use in 1173, but we can probably allow this weapon a lifetime previous to that of 30 years—or why not 50, or even 70?—so we do not get a late, terminating date for the making of the type. Actual specimens of it may still have been in use a century or more later.

Many other swords of Type XI have similar inscriptions inlaid in white or yellow metal, one in the National Museum of Denmark at Copenhagen (plate 4C) being of almost the same shape and dimensions as the runic sword in my collection. Of the specimens so far found, only a few have iron inlays like the six Gicelin swords (two are in the City Museum at Lincoln) the majority having finely made religious inlays in the style of the Fornham sword. But as in all these types, new examples are constantly being dug up, or identified, and more information about the type as a whole will undoubtedly come to light.

The form of these swords is clearly defined, classic examples

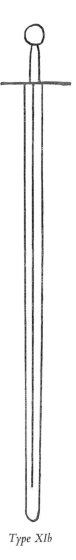

Type XIb

<hr />

[28] Wegeli, op. cit.

[29] e.g. two in the British Museum; one from Little Bealings, Suffolk, another from the Thames at Wandsworth; a third from Sittingbourne in Kent (B.M. "Guide to Anglo-Saxon and Viking Antiquities"; and *The Sword in Anglo-Saxon England*, Dr. H. R. E. Davidson), and a fourth from London (London Museum).

[30] There is a fragment of a sword in the London Museum which has, inlaid in latten on one side of the blade, an interlacing pattern of the same character as those on the reverse of some of the Ulfberht blades. Found in the Thames. Layton Collection.

being shown on plate 3, but as in all these sword-types, there are many survivors which do not conform. One such is in the Museum of Ethnology and Archaeology at Cambridge,[31] the other in the Armouries of the Tower of London.[32] Both have very broad blades which are otherwise of the general shape of Type XI; both have very narrow fullers, running nearly full-length, as in XI. The Cambridge sword has a flat disc pommel and a short, slightly curved cross while the Tower one has a small, roughly-shaped nut pommel and a short straight cross, as in many XI's (plate 5A and C). Though there are few of these, we may put them into a sub-type and call it XIa.

Several other swords appear to be of Type XI, but have rather shapeless blades, narrow, parallel sided with little or no taper, and cut off at the tip to an almost square point. It does not seem certain that in each case the actual point itself is broken off. Some appear to have been made like that, so much so that we may place them as a sub-type also, calling it XIb.[33]

Swords of Type XI seem rarely to be shown in art. The early,

Fig. 13. From a panel on one of the 11th century bronze doors of St. Zeno Cathedral, Verona.

[31] Cat. 76 22.731.

[32] Armouries, Tower of London, acquired 1961. Sotheby's, April 28th, 1961, Lot 145.

[33] Examples are in the Nat. Museum of Denmark, Copenhagen, in the collection of Mr. E. A. Christensen of Copenhagen; Bruhn Hoffmeyer, pl. Vg, p. 8; and in the Bernische Historische Museum at Berne (Cat. no. 226.7).

Anglo-Saxon examples already mentioned are perhaps the clearest; some of the swords wielded by Harold's warriors on the Bayeux Tapestry could be of this type, but the character of that document forbids too close a reliance upon detail. There is a figure embossed on one of the leaves of the great bronze doors of the church of St. Zeno at Verona (fig. 13) which has what appears to be one, but one would hesitate to say definitely that the many swords apparently of Type XI shown in many manuscripts of the 11–12th centuries are indeed such. They are just swords.

TYPE XII CHARACTERISTICS

A broad, flat, evenly tapering *blade*, generally with a good sharp point and tending to widen perceptibly below the hilt. The *fuller* is well-marked and occupies $\frac{2}{3}$ to $\frac{3}{4}$ of the blade-length. It often starts on the tang within the hilt, and may be double or treble. The *grip* is a little longer than in the preceding types, averaging about $4\frac{1}{2}''$. The *tang* is generally flat with almost parallel sides, or swelling a little in the middle. The *cross* can be of almost any style, though a short, straight one is most common. The *pommel*, too, can be of any type though the thick disc with strongly bevelled edges (Type I) predominates.

General Remarks

At the time of writing there is no sword of this type which can give any indication of a date for its earliest use. The only datable example is a late one—the splendid sword, surely the most perfect example of the knightly sword to survive (plates 7 and 9) found in 1943 in Toledo Cathedral[34] in the grave of Sancho IV, el Bravo, King of Castile and Leon from 1284 to 1295. A similar though much plainer sword was found in the tomb of Sancho's elder brother, Fernando de la Cerda (in the chapel of the monastery of las Huelgas at Burgos) who died in 1270.[35] This one is still in its scabbard and cannot therefore be positively listed as a Type XII sword, though the outline of the sheath and the proportions of the whole suggest that it is (plate 10). The sword of El Bravo gives a terminus ante quem of 1295, that of Fernando of 1270, neither of

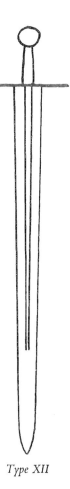

Type XII

[34] London, Journal of the Arms and Armour Society, 1959. Blair, Claude, "Medieval Swords and Spurs Preserved in Toledo Cathedral"; and Oakeshott, *The Archaeology of Weapons*, op. cit., pp. 245-7, frontis. and plate 10a.
[35] Gomez-Moreno, Manuel, *El Panteon Real de las Huelgas de Burgos*, 1946.

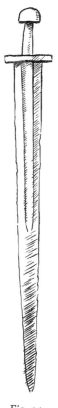

which dates is really helpful. A considerably later, though similar-looking, sword lay from 1329 until 1921 in the coffin of Can Grande della Scala, Lord of Verona, at which latter date it was removed to the Museo Archaeologico of that city, where it has ever since been mouldering away[36] (plate 46A). It may be a XII, but the blade will now never be seen unless an X-ray photograph can be taken, and the proportions of the whole thing suggest that it could belong to Type XIII, although by 1329 swords of Type XVI had been in use for some time, particularly in Italy, so we must not accept this otherwise intensely interesting weapon as an example of any type.

A great many specimens of Type XII survive, some in splendid condition, but none can give any date, even the vague one of a tomb or battlefield find. Their blades show a great variety of inlaid inscriptions, running the whole gamut of those which were popular between 1200 and 1350,[37] and a good many makers' marks, a feature which, since the well-marked blades of the 1st to 6th centuries,[38] has not been found in any of the earlier medieval swords—disregarding, of course, the actual smith-names. A few, such as an almost identical pair, one in London[39] and the other in Berne,[40] have pommels of a kind which tempt us to give them a date within the 11th century (fig. 1).

Fig. 14.
Type X, or XII?

There are, of course, unplaceable swords which at first sight look as though they should belong to the type, but which have irregular features. There is in Zurich[41] a sword which looks like, and has indeed always been assumed to be, a Viking sword of Type VIIIa; yet it has an absolutely classic Type XII blade (fig. 14). Is the blade just an unusual one for the Viking age, or is the hilt a late, 13th century survival of a Viking type? Then there is that remarkable sword preserved in almost pristine condition in the

[36] The photograph reproduced on plate 46A was made when the sword was newly taken from the coffin. Its condition now has badly deteriorated. It has been published previously only in *The Archaeology of Weapons*, op. cit., chap. 17, p. 307.

[37] Wegeli, op. cit.

[38] Davidson, *The Sword in Anglo-Saxon England*, op. cit. Oakeshott, *The Archaeology of Weapons*, op. cit., chap. 6, pp. 99–100.

[39] Armouries of the Tower of London, acquired 1961. Sotheby's, April 28th, 1961, Lot 141.

[40] Bernische Historische Museum, Cat. No. 840.5. The hilts of these two swords are similar to an Ulfberht sword, *c.* 950, in the Mus. Hamb. Gesch., 31. Bruhn Hoffmeyer, pl. IVd, p. 7.

[41] Zweizerisches Landesmuseum, Cat. No. 15672. Bruhn Hoffmeyer, pl. IVb, p. 7.

Armeria Reale at Turin, another weapon attributed to St. Maurice.[42] Its blade has a well-marked fuller, about $\frac{1}{3}$ of the blade's width, running to within a few inches of a rather sharp point. At a glance, the sword looks like one of those long X's, for it has a Brazil-nut pommel of a popular 11th–12th century form; its cross is undatable, for it is of a kind often used up to the second quarter of the 15th century, though examples may be found on swords which seem to date in the 13th or 12th centuries, and it was known in Scandinavia early in the 11th[43]—in fact, it is almost identical, except for the decoration, with the cross on Sancho IV's sword. So is the Turin St. Maurice sword a late example of Type X, or one of Type XII? There are many of the earlier swords, including some of Types VIII and VII which have blades remarkably similar in size, balance and weight to this one. Unless some piece of internal evidence hitherto unnoticed comes to light, we shall never be able to be certain.

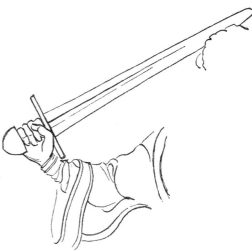

Fig. 15. St. Michael, Bamberg Cathedral, c. 1220.

To obtain dates for the earliest and (perhaps) the latest use of Type XII we must turn to its portrayal in art. The fine drawings in the Winchester Bible (c. 1170)[44] show swords which may be meant to be of the type, though the blades are too vaguely drawn to be certain. However, a figure of the Archangel Michael in Bamberg Cathedral (fig. 15) shows a perfect example—incidentally with a hilt identical with those swords in London and Berne mentioned above and illustrated in fig. 1. This sculpture can be dated at around 1200,[45] or perhaps a year or two after. After this, nearly every sword shown in monumental sculpture for the next 80 years is a XII. There are so many of these that it

[42] Laking, op. cit., vol. I, chap. III, fig. 108, p. 86.

[43] Petersen, De Norske Vikingesverd, op. cit., p. 168, fig. 130, p. 172, fig. 133a, p. 179, fig. 138; and Copenhagen Nat. Mus., a sword with no inventory number.

[44] Oakeshott, W. F., The Artists of the Winchester Bible, 1945.

[45] Pinder, W., Der Bamberger Dom, 1937. A very similar hilt is shown in a sculpture in Wechselburg Cathedral of Abraham about to sacrifice Isaac.

Fig. 16. Dietrich von Brehna, Naumburg Cathedral, c. 1250. Type XII sheathed.

is impossible to list them all.[46] Many of these sculptured swords (as figs. 16 and 17) are sheathed, but there are a great many drawn ones in the hands of innumerable St. Peters (fig. 18), St. Pauls, St. Georges, St. Michaels, and show clear examples of the type.

The same may be said of manuscript illustration. Undoubtedly the best, and the best known, are the pictures in the "Maciejowski Bible"[47] made in about 1250, and many may be seen in an Apocalypse, made about 20 years earlier, in the library of Trinity College, Cambridge.[48] For later examples we have a "Romance of Alexander" made in about 1330 (Bodleian Library, Oxford)[49] which shows many Type XII swords in company with others of XIII, XIV and XV. This is because the manuscript was illustrated in that period when armour was in transition from mail to plate, and new types of sword were evolved to cope with it. It could be said that when this transition was completed, the old flat, light, cutting blade had become obsolete, but it seems not to have been so. In spite of the introduction of new types of sword better suited to over-

[46] Perhaps the finest sculptured examples are to be seen on the south porch of Chartres Cathedral (*c.* 1230) and on the west front of Notre Dame de Paris (*c.* 1250). In Germany there are so many it is difficult to select the best—the figures so plentifully carved in the Cathedral of Freiburg (*c.* 1300), and the statues of the Benefactors of Naumburg (*c.* 1260). Many German tomb effigies show them also. Many photographs of these sculptures are in *Die Denkmaler der Deutsche Bildauerkunst*, by G. Dehio and G. V. Bezold, I and II; and *Die Sculpturen von Frieburg and Wechselburg*, by A. Goldschmidt. There are so many excellent books on German medieval sculpture that they cannot be listed in a note. A fuller list is given in the Bibliography.

[47] A manuscript of Old Testament Stories, French? *c.* 1250, given in the 17th century by Cardinal Bernard Maciejowski to Shah Abbas the Great of Persia. Now in the Pierpont Morgan Library in New York.

[48] Trinity College, Cambridge. MS. R.16.2.

[49] James, M. R., *The Romance of Alexander*, a facsimile of MS. Bodley 264. Oxford, 1933.

come the protection afforded by plate armour, there can be no doubt that the outmoded sword-types continued in use. With the next two types, perhaps the next three, we reach a point where it would seem that a sword-form was being sought which would be more effective against the very efficient armour worn during the years between *c*. 1275–1325.

TYPE XIII CHARACTERISTICS

A broad *blade*, nearly as wide at the tip as at the hilt. Most examples show a distinct widening immediately below the hilt, thereafter the edges run with an imperceptible taper to a spatulate point. The fuller generally occupies a little more than half of the blade's length. The *grip* is long in proportion to the blade—average length 6″. The *tang* may be flat and broad, tapering sharply in its upper half towards the pommel, or it may be of a thick rectangular or square section, giving the appearance of being thin and stalk-like when seen in elevation. The *pommel* may be of any type, though on most surviving specimens Types D, E and I are the most common (the developed late Brazil-nut forms or the so-called "wheel" form). The *cross* is generally straight, though there are a few curved examples.

Fig. 17. Count Ekkehard, Naumburg, c. 1250.

Type XIII

General Remarks

Specimens of this type are rare. There is no positive dating evidence. A very fine sword found on the site of a battle fought in 1234 at Altenesch, near Oldenburg[50], may be of this type, but the last few inches of the point are broken off and it cannot positively be said that it is not a XII. However, we find several examples in art which give

[50] Z.H.W.K. Band XI, p. 220. Oldenburg, *Jahrbuch des Vereins für Altertumskunde und Landesgesch.*, 1926, p. 162ff.; and Bruhn Hoffmeyer, plate XIVc, p. 22.

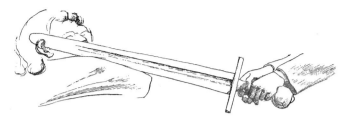

Fig. 18. St. Peter. Naumburg, c. 1250. Type XII unsheathed.

the date between about 1260 and 1310; but it is the far more important sub-type, XIIIa, which gives us ample and convincing evidence that both type and sub-types belong to the period 1240–1350.

SUB-TYPE XIIIA CHARACTERISTICS

This is generally the same shape as Type XIII, only much larger. The *blade*, of similar form, is generally from 37″ to 40″ long, while the *grip* ranges from 6½″ to 9″ in length.

General Remarks

The size of a sword has not hitherto determined its type, but here, and in swords of the 14th and 15th centuries, it will be found to do so. The reason here is partly that the XIIIa's are very big weapons, partly because in their own time they were distinguished from their smaller contemporaries by the term "espées de Guerre" or "Grete Swerdes".

This statement must be examined in detail.[51] In the literature of the late 13th and early 14th centuries we find many references to these "espées de guerre", "Grant espées", "Grete Swerdes", and so on. In art of the same period we find many portrayals of very large swords of Type XIIIa, and there are a considerable number of survivors. The references to "Grete Swerdes" do not, I believe, indicate two-hand swords, for these are always described as such, as "espées a deux mains" or "Twahandswerds", and need not be confused with the sword of war. The two-hander of the 13th–15th centuries was not, as in the 16th, a specialised form of weapon; it was just an outsize specimen; in the late 13th and the 14th

---

[51] A note published in 1954 in the Journal of the Arms and Armour Society, vol. I, No. 8. R. E. Oakeshott, "A War Sword of the XIVth Century in the Guildhall Museum"

centuries of Types XII or XIIIa, and in the 15th of Types XV or XVIII.

Froissart, writing of the Canon de Robesart under the year 1358, says: "Il tenoit une espée a deuz mains, dont il donnoit les horions si grands que nul les osoit attendre"[52] and in the Chronicle of Du Guesclin we read:[53]

> "Oliver de Manny le fere tellement
> D'une espée a II mains, qui tranchoit roidement:
> Sur le col du cheval l'espée si descent
> Tellement l'assena que la teste lue fent."

An earlier example of the use of a two-hander is found in a Romance of Alexander of c. 1180:[54] "Il trait le bone espée a II espieus molus" and a later reference is in the will of Sir John Deepdene (1402):[55] "Unum gladium ornatum cum argento et j. twahandswerd".

Thus it seems that the war-sword was not regarded as a two-hander. What other, then, can it be but this very big sword of a kind which, in its later forms, is familiar as the Bastard or hand-and-a-half sword? We find it distinguished in a class of its own, for instance, in the inventory of the effects of Humphrey de Bohun (ob. 1319) made in 1322:[56] "III espées: l'un des armes le dit counte, lautre de Seint George, et le tierce sarziney: le quarte de guerre".[57] In 1305 Guillaume Guiart writes of

> ". . . Grans espées d'Allemagne
> leur tranchant souvent les poins outre."

We meet these "big swords of Germany" a good deal earlier. Primatus[58] describing the battle of Benevento in 1266, tells of the

[52] Hewitt, John, *Ancient Armour and Weapons in Europe*, 3 vols. London, 1855–60. Vol. II, p. 256.

[53] Hewitt, op. cit., vol. II, p. 256.

[54] Victor Gay, *Glossaire Archaeologique du Moyen Age et de la Renaissance*, 2 vols., Paris, 1887 and 1928, vol. I, p. 644.

[55] Hewitt, op. cit., vol. II, p. 256.

[56] Hewitt, op. cit., vol. II, p. 246.

[57] Hewitt, op. cit., vol. I, p. 311.

[58] Primatus, in Martin Bouquet, *Recueil des Historiens des Gaules et de France*, XX, 28. "Les Francois boutoient les espées grilles et agues sous les esselles d'icentre, on ils apparoient touz désarmés, et les transpercoient si tort comme il levoient les bras pour ferir, et leur boutoient les espées parmi les entrailles." And Clericus Parisiensis in Mod. Germ., XXVI, 582: "Clamatum est a parte nostra quod in hoste de ensibus percuterent destoc."

Type XIIIa

43

great slashing swords of the German mercenaries of Manfred of Sicily. He also mentions the fact that these men wore plate-armour, which was then in Germany beginning to come into fashion. Incidentally, in describing the battle he tells how the French knights had great difficulty with this strong and solid body of horsemen; their swords made no impression on this armour until some observant knight noticed that when the Germans lifted their great swords to strike, a vulnerable place appeared under their arms. A cry went up to use the point (à l'estoc) and stab under the arm; soon a number of Germans were disabled in this way by the French swords, which were shorter and more acutely pointed than those of the Germans.[59] These were perhaps of Type XIV, to be examined next.

The expression "Grant Espée" would distinguish Types XIIIa from the "epée courte" or "parvus ensis" which may have been the short weapon of Types XIV or XV, better known by its 15th century name of "arming sword".[60] This distinction does not occur before the second half of the 13th century, though it is frequent after. In the will of Odo de Rousillon (1298) we have "meum magnum cultellum, et meam parvam ensem". Again, Guiart writing under the year 1301, says

"Les Francois espées reportent
Courte et roides, dont ils taillent."

Included among the arms and armour provided by Thomas de Erskyn for a duel in 1368 were "unum cultellum, unum ensem longum, unum ensem curtum". Much later, in the 1450's, we find the same distinction between the long sword and the short one, and the carrying of both in a duel. ". . . He daggere upon hys righte side. And then hys shorte swerde upon hys lyfte syde in a rounde rynge all nakid to pulle it out lightli . . . and then hys long swerd in hys hande."[61]

---

[59] ibid. See also Oman, Sir Charles, *A History of the Art of War in the Middle Ages*, London, 1928. Vol. I, p. 503.

[60] "Led. Pelerin dit qu'il portait . . . une très belle espées d'armes . . ." (Proces. P. Pelerin (1431) Gay, op. cit., vol. I, p. 645.)

[61] From a treatise of *c.* 1450 included in the Hastings MS, on "How a man schal be armyd at his ese when he schal fighte on foote". Viscount Dillon, "On a MS collection of Ordinances of Chivalry of the Fifteenth century, belonging to Lord Hastings". Archaeologia, Vol. LVII, 1900, p. 44.

Even so, there are many references to a second sword being carried at the saddle, as well as one at the waist, though no distinction is ever made as to their size. For instance the "Roman de Rou" (c. 1170) has:

"Li Dus fist cheval demander,
Plusors en fist tres li mener;
Chescun on a l'arcon devant
Une espée bone pendant."[62]

Fig. 19. From the Tenison Psalter, English, before 1284.

and the Sieur de Joinville, writing in 1309 of an incident in the battle of Mansourah in St. Louis' fatal crusade of 1250, tells how a Saracen horseman charged at him from the side, and bore him down across his horse's neck, and says: "et me coucha sur le col de mon cheval, et me tint si pressé que je ne pouvoie traire l'espée que j'avoie ceinte. Si me convint traire l'espée qui estoit a mon cheval."[63] Then, later still in 1372 D'Orronville describes ". . . David Olegreve qui . . . portait deux espées, une ceinte et l'autre a l'arcon de la selle".[64] It seems reasonable to suppose that these big "war swords" may have been carried in this way, and yet it is curious that in spite of these literary references to a sword at the saddle bow, it seems to be nowhere represented in art. On the other hand, there are many showing swords of Type XIIIa at the knightly belt. Datable ones, too. Fig. 19 shows one admirably. This is a miniature from a psalter made before 1284 for the short-lived prince Alfonso (a son of Edward I of England), who died in that year.[65] This pictured sword may be compared with those shown in plate 14. Another English manuscript, an Apocalypse of St. John made c. 1300–1310,[66] shows many of these great swords

[62] Roman de Rou (1170). Gay, op. cit., vol. I, p. 644.

[63] Gay, op. cit., vol. II, p. 644.

[64] D'Orronville, "Vie de Louis de Bourbon", c. 38. Hewitt, op. cit., vol. II, 353.

[65] "The Tenison Psalter", B.M. MS. Add. 24636.

[66] B.M. MS. Roy. 19. B.XV.

45

worn at the belt (fig. 20). A sculpture where we might reasonably have expected to see the sword hanging from the saddle is the little figure on the canopy of the tomb of Edmund, Earl of Lancaster, in Westminster Abbey[67] (*ob.* 1296), yet it is at his belt (fig. 21).

There are a great many of these swords, some of Type XIII and some of XIIIa, on the sculptured figures in Freiburg Cathedral, all made between about 1295 and 1310.

We do not often see these great swords on tomb effigies. There are a few in Germany dating in the 1340's and 50's,[68] and there are

Fig. 20. *From an Apocalypse of St. John, English, c. 1300.*

at least two in England, one of rather small proportions on the figure of a knight *c.* 1350 in the church at Puddletown in Dorset, and another full-sized one on the effigy of Sir Oliver Ingham (+1343) at Ingham in Norfolk. (This may be of Type XVIa or XVII. (A third is on the figure of Sir John de Ifield (*c.* 1325) at Ifield, Sussex. We may perhaps take it, since there are as many references to "swords of war" as there are to "great swords" and since both seem to indicate the same sort of weapon, that it was indeed so— the type was used in war, and was not the everyday sword of the knight such as might be shown on his monument.

Fig. 21. *From the canopy of the tomb of Edmund Crouchback, Westminster Abbey, 1296.*

However, there are many effigies in England showing swords with very

[67] Illustrated in Stothard, *Monumental Effigies.*
[68] e.g. at Bopfingen, Westphalia (1359).

large blades, which, though sheathed, by their outline suggest Type XIII blades; but they have hilts of a more normal size, only about 5″ long in spite of the very long blades. It would seem that here is another sub-type of XIII.

SUB-TYPE XIIIB CHARACTERISTICS

The *blade* is similar to Type XIII, though in some cases may be narrower. The hilt is similar, but the *grip* is of the ordinary, short one-handed length.

General Remarks

There are more sculptured examples of this sub-type than there are survivors. The most notable in English effigies are those on the brasses of the two Sir John D'Abernons (1277 and 1327)[69], Sir Robert de Septvans[70] (1306), Sir ? Fitzralph [71] (1323) and Sir John de Creke[72] (1326), and the effigies of an Astbury at Astbury in Cheshire[73] (1300) and of a de Montfort at Hitchendon, Bucks (*c.* 1290).[74]

It does not seem likely that because a sword of this kind has a very large blade, it can be classified as a great sword, any more than it can be if it has a long grip. It has to have both long grip *and* big blade together to qualify for the title.

There are a few survivors of Type XIII (for example, one in the Tower of London),[75] many of XIIIa and several of XIIIb. No complete sword can be dated, but there is a very good blade, without any hilt, which has all the classic characteristics of the type, in the Kunsthistorisches Museum at Vienna.[76] By the arms engraved upon it, this blade has been confidently attributed to the ownership of Ottokar II, king of Bohemia from 1258–1278, and so can be dated between those years. A later example—or,

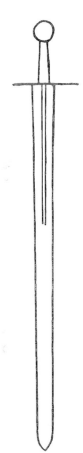

Type XIIIb

[69] In the church at Stoke d'Abernon, Surrey. Sir John the Younger (+1327) is illustrated in Stothard's *Monumental Effigies*.

[70] Chartham, Kent.

[71] Pebmarsh, Essex.

[72] Westley Waterless, Cambridge.

[73] Astbury, Cheshire.

[74] Hitchendon, Bucks. Stothard, *Monumental Effigies*.

[75] On loan from the collection of the late Sir James Mann.

[76] Inv. no. A.34. Jahrbuch der K. H. Museum in Wien, Band 57.1961; Gamber, Ortwin, *Die Mittelalterlichen Blankwaffen der Wiener Waffensammlung*, p. 16–18, fig. 12.

rather, a battlefield find which may provide a terminus ante quem—is in the National Museum at Copenhagen.[77] This is a good specimen, almost identical in shape and size with a sword of the type found in the Thames in London, and was found on the site of the battle fought at Nonnebjerg in Denmark in 1340. The dates of these two correspond with the evidence of the monuments. Examples of the type and sub-types are shown in plates 11 to 14. Of Type XIII, one of the best (plate 11B) is in the Armouries of the Tower of London. The grip is long in proportion to the blade, which has all the characteristics of the type. Inlaid in the fuller is the well-known mark of the "running wolf", in subsequent centuries so familiar as a mark of the smiths of Solingen and Passau. It seems first to have been used late in the 13th century. One of the most notable examples of Type XIIIa was found in the Thames off the Temple in London and is now in the Guildhall Museum.[78] This one has a bladesmith's mark in the blade just below the hilt, a little dagger inlaid in latten (fig. 22). Another even finer sword from the same workshop is in the collection of Mr. R. T. Gwynn of Epsom (Type XVIa). This sword is of absolutely outstanding quality, being in almost pristine condition. It has previously been published,[79] and is generally held to belong to the late 14th century, but I believe it should be dated within its first half. Its blade is a little more slender than the Guildhall one, but that need surely not be any indication of later date. Another very fine, well-preserved sword of this type used to be in the collection of M. Charles Boissonas at Geneva.[80] Here the blade is even narrower, but the marks upon it (fig. 23) are of a character[81] unlikely to be of a date later than 1350. The pommel, too, is of an unusual form, a cube with the corners bevelled off.

Fig. 22. Mark on a XIIIa blade, Guildhall, London.

Fig. 23. Marks on a XIIIa blade, ex. Boissonas Collection.

Several swords of Type XIIIa are in Stockholm with these pommels,[82] but the only one clearly shown in art is on an English effigy of c. 1320, at Halton Holgate in Lincolnshire (fig. 70). There is another very fine XIIIa in Berne[83] and a similar one used to be

[77] Inv. no. D.10172. Hoffmeyer, op. cit., vol. II, p. 16 and plate XVF.
[78] Oakeshott, Journal of the Arms and Armour Society. op. cit.
[79] ibid., and Connoisseur Year Book, 1954.
[80] Boissonas, C., *Armes Anciennes de la Suisse*, Plate Xb.
[81] Wegeli, *Inschriften*, op. cit.
[82] Stockholm, National Historical Museum. Inv. Nos. 23454, 13580.
[83] Bernische Historische Museum. Inv. No. 226.2.

in the Boissonas Collection,[84] and another is in my own possession[85] (plate 13).

Some early examples of war swords have pommels of the later Brazil-nut forms. There is a very fine one in the Fitzwilliam Museum in Cambridge,[86] another in the Musée Masséna at Nice[87], and a third in the collection at Kreutzenstein.[88] All of these, by their pommels, suggest a date within the third quarter of the 13th century. One of the figures of the Benefactors of Naumburg Cathedral (Count Herrmann), c. 1260, has a pommel very similar to the Nice example, on a great sword of Type XIIIa.

There are two good examples of XIIIb in Britain, and a superlative one in Spain. The first is in the Wallace Collection in London[89] (plate 19A). The blade of this sword is of particularly fine quality as well as being of an unusual section. It has a fuller running right to the point, very deep and well-marked, and the faces of the blade between the sides of this fuller and the edges of the blade are strongly hollowed. There is no visible smith's mark. The hilt is quite plain, and the whole sword is of particularly fine proportions. The blade is $33\frac{3}{4}''$ long. Of identical proportions but much smaller size—it is a boy's sword—is the beautiful little weapon preserved in Toledo Cathedral. The arms upon its pommel and scabbard-mounts suggest that it belonged to the Infante Don Juan —el de Tarifa—a son of Alfonso X of Castile. This prince was killed at an early age in 1319, so the sword was probably made early in the 14th century (plate 17).

Another example is in my own collection. The blade shows no less than three unusual features. It is of fairly small proportions, being rather slender; its section is six-sided (foreshadowing the most common blade-section of the second half of the 14th century); it has a strongly built-up shoulder at the top of the

---

[84] Boissonas, op. cit., pl. Xc.

[85] Oakeshott, *The Archaeology of Weapons*, op. cit., p. 250–1, plate 9a.

[86] Illustrated in *Arms and Armour of England*, Mann, Sir James, London, 1960, plate 4c.

[87] Laking, *A Record for European Armour and Arms*, op. cit., Vol. I, p. 84, fig. 104.

[88] Illustrated in *Erinnerungen Eines Waffénsammlers*, Graf Wilczec, Vienna, 1908. Abb. 28.

[89] Wallace Collection no. A459 (old No. 4); Bruhn Hoffmeyer, pl. XVIa, p. 18.

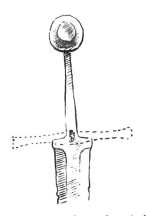

blade which fits into a slot in the cross,[90] and stamped deeply into the tang is a fine mark, the "wild man" or "Wodewose" which is so familiar as a swordsmith's mark in the 16th and 17th centuries.[91] Here we find it quite clearly in a sword of undoubted early 14th century date. The cross is short and straight, of circular section widening at the ends (style 2) and the large, well-formed pommel is of Type I, of deep

Fig. 24. XIIIb sword, author's wheel form (fig. 24). Another with a
collection. developed Brazil-nut pommel of Type D is in the Royal Scottish Museum in Edinburgh (plate 12B), and yet another, found in the Rhine, is in the collection of Mr. C. O. von Kienbusch in New York.

In the same collection is a particularly bold example of XIIIb, which has its almost exact counterpart in the Christensen Collection in Denmark (plate 12A). Both these swords are distinguished by having similar smiths' marks and Arabic inscriptions on their blades.[92] These inscriptions, later additions to the blade, record that they were placed in the Hall of Victories in the Arsenal of Alexandria in 1368—presumably as trophies taken by the Mameluke Sultans of Egypt from the forces of Peter of Lusignan, King of Cyprus and titular king of Jerusalem, after the defeat of his abortive assault on Cairo in 1365.

The "swords of war" of Type XIIIa are indeed admirably adapted for the work they had to do—to deal slow, ponderous slashing blows from the back of a horse at a well-protected adversary some distance away. They may have been developed as some kind of answer to the avowedly more efficient armour of this period at the start of the transition from mail to plate, when certain reinforcements were worn over the mail, such as poleyns

[90] This feature, so common in sword blades of the 16th and 17th centuries, was used frequently in the 2nd-5th centuries A.D. and intermittently all through the Middle Ages. See Bronsted, J., *Danmarks Oldtid*, I–III, 1938–40; Engelhardt, C. Vimosefundet, 1869; Oakeshott, op. cit., p. 99, fig. 39.

[91] The mark associated with the name of Johannes Hoppe in the 17th century.

[92] Catalogue, the Kretschmar von Kienbusch Collection. Princeton University, 1963, No. 324. Combe, Et. and De Cosson, A.F.C., *European Swords with Arabic Inscriptions*, Bull. de la Soc. Royale d'Arch. d'Alexandrie, 31, 1937.

and couters, greaves and plated gauntlets; and under it, coats-of-plates and "cuiries". As we shall see in examining the next few types, there were various efforts made during the first half of the 14th century to cope with improvements in armour. This, which was simply an extension of the age-old idea of smiting an adversary with mighty, shearing blows by providing an even stouter and heavier cutting blade, may have been the first.

TYPE XIV CHARACTERISTICS

A short, broad and sharply-pointed *blade*, tapering strongly from the hilt, of flat section (the point end of the blade may, in some examples, have a slight though perceptible mid-rib—see plate 20A), with a fuller running about half, or a little over, of its length. This may be single and quite broad, or multiple and narrow. The *grip* is generally short (average $3\frac{3}{4}''$) though some are as long as $4\frac{1}{2}''$;[93] the *tang* is thick and parallel-sided, often with the fuller extending half-way up it. The *pommel* is always of "wheel" form, sometimes very wide and flat (Type K) but generally of the commoner Type I. The *cross* is generally rather long and curved (very rarely straight) of styles 6 or 7.

General Remarks

So far there is no example of this type which can give a date, though several have inlaid letters which suggest the period 1270–1340. Representations in art are very frequent, often very carefully drawn or sculpted, during the same period. The type seems to have been most popular in France, Italy and England. German examples are rare, though many are shown in a manuscript of

Type XIV

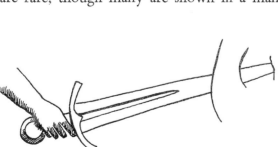

Fig. 25. From a roof boss, Angel Choir, Lincoln Cathedral, c. 1280.

[93] For instance, a sword in the City Museum at Lincoln.

Fig. 26. A "Deposition from the Cross", Lucca Cathedral, by Nicola Pisano, 1258–78.

c. 1330, with swords of the more typical German Type XIIIa.[94] By its form and date one might suppose that this was the type of sword Primatus speaks of when he describes the fight at Benevento in 1266. An excellent portrayal of one is in the Angel Choir of Lincoln Cathedral (datable at *c.* 1280) (fig. 25), and another which only shows the hilt and the tip of the short scabbarded blade is in a marble panel over a door in the Cathedral at Lucca by Nicola Pisano (a Deposition from the Cross, fig. 26), 1258–78.[95] This is particularly interesting since it is identical in form and proportion with a sword (fig. 27) found in Switzerland, now in the Zweizerisches Landesmuseum at Zurich.[96] Another well-defined example is on the effigy in the Abbey of St. Denis of Count Robert of Artois, who died in 1317[97] (fig. 28). In fact, there are so many shown in monuments dating between *c.* 1310 and 1330 in Alsace and the Rhineland—all the effigies of the Landgraves of Hesse in the church of St. Elizabeth at Marburg have them—that it is pointless to try and list them.[98] Nearly all English effigies of this period,[99] too, have these swords, though in all these cases a certain amount of caution is needed: they are all in their scabbards, and so may be of Types XV or XVI which have similar silhouettes but a different blade-section.[100]

Actual survivals are not very common. The best is in the Metropolitan Museum of Art in New York (plate 16). This is an

[94] The "Willehalms Codex" in Cassel. Published in facsimile by C. Freyhan in Leipzig, 1925–27.

[95] A cast of this may be seen in the Victoria and Albert Museum in London.

[96] Inv. no. IN 6982. Illustrated in a Zweizerisches Landesmuseum publication, "Schwerter und Degen", Dr. Hugo Schneider. No. 7.

[97] Illustrated in Hamann, R., *Die Elizabeths Kirche zu Marburg*, vol. II, "Die Plastike", Marburg, 1929.

[98] Ibid.

[99] For instance, the brass of Sir Robert de Bures, Acton, Suffolk (1302), Edmund, Earl of Lancaster, in Westminster Abbey (1296); Sir Richard de Whatton (*c.* 1310) at Whatton, Notts.; an unknown knight at Gosberton, Lincs. (*c.* 1310), and many others.

[100] The effigy of William Longespee the younger, *c.* 1280, in Salisbury Cathedral, shows the sword partly drawn from the scabbard. The blade is of a four-sided, flattened diamond section, as in Type XV (see fig. 29 below).

absolutely outstanding weapon, of the very finest quality and in pristine condition. The inscription upon the pommel, which is engraved on a band of silver set on to the outer flange of it, reads: Sunt hic etiam sua praecuna laudi (Here also are the Heralds of His praise). There seem to be the remains, in the fuller, of inscriptions of a kind dated by Wegeli in the second half of the 13th century. Another good example is in my own collection[101] (plate 19B) and a third shown in fig. 27 is in Zurich.[102] Others are in Lincoln and in the collection of Mr. J. Pocock (plate 20C), and in Berne.[103]

With Type XIV we come to the end of the types in Group I, the swords with flat, light blades designed primarily for cutting, and to oppose armour of mail. The swords of Group II to be examined now are all of a stiffer section, with blades effective for thrusting, often with reinforced and very acute points, designed to oppose the armour of plate prevalent after 1350. It must not be assumed, however, that the light flat blade went out of use.

In the Levant and Southern Europe the wearing of full plate armour was never so thoroughly adopted as in the west and north, maybe because of the climate. So the cutting blade would still be useful. This is shown by several swords upon whose blades are Arabic inscriptions which tell us that they were captured in various campaigns by the Mameluke rulers of Egypt—some from an abortive Christian attack on Cairo led by Peter of Lusignan, titular king of Jerusalem, in 1365 and others in a vic-

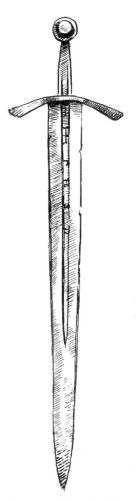

Fig. 27. Type XIV sword, Landesmuseum, Zurich, c. 1300, cf. fig. 26.

---

[101] Described in *The Archaeology of Weapons*, p. 230, plates 7d and 8c.
[102] Zweizerisches Landesmuseum, Inv. no. IN 6982. See note 96 above.
[103] Bernische Historische Museum, Inv. no. 851.

torious raid on Cyprus made by Malik al-asraf Barsabay in 1426. These captured swords were hung up in the Hall of Victories in the arsenal of Alexandria, and inscribed sometimes with a date (e.g. 1367–8 for trophies of de Lusignan's raid) and sometimes simply with the name of the Emir in charge of the arsenal at the time when the inscription was made. This is generally as good as a date, for few of these Emirs seem to have held their posts for longer than a year or so. Several swords, unfortunately, have very vague legends on them which give neither names nor dates. However, it is three of these swords which interest us here, though we shall hear more of them later. Two identical weapons, one in the collection of Mr. C. O. von Kienbusch in New York and the other (plate 12A) in the collection of Mr. E. A. Christensen of Copenhagen, have very broad blades of Type XIIIb, yet they are dated 1368 and were (presumably) used in 1365. This, of course, does not in any way suggest that they were made as late as 1365, or even one or two decades earlier. Though there is a certain amount of literary evidence that swords in the later Middle Ages were used by successive generations of men as they were in the Migration and Viking periods,[104] it is reasonable to assume they had a lifetime of half a century or so. The third is a big sword of type XIIIa in the Royal Ontario Museum at Toronto; it is dated 1427. Though it has the classic proportions of Type XIIIa, its hilt is of a form which we shall meet again in dealing with the swords of the 15th century. The pommel is flat and rectangular, and the cross is long, slender and has the ends curved horizontally into a flat S shape. The blade has three fullers, and does not widen at all at the hilt. The whole sword is in fact singularly ugly, but extremely interesting as being a late example of Type XIIIa. The hilt is of a kind which seems to have become popular late in the 14th century, very many examples of which have been found in Hungary, and still more in Venetian territory; there are literally hundreds of them in the Arsenal at Venice. This may be a late example of Type XIIIa, but is by no means the latest. It seems to have become very popular again during the last quarter of the 15th century, judging by the number of specimens there are of

[104] References to this in the Sagas are too numerous to mention here, but good examples are to be found in Volsungasaga, Grettis Saga, Viga Glums Saga and Laxdaela Saga.

this period. Many have 15th century blades, but there are many with old blades of the 13th–14th century—as can be told by the marks and inlays on them—which have been fitted with hilts of a kind which were up-to-date between 1475 and 1525. A very good example of the former is in the Museum and Art Gallery, Glasgow, and of the latter the famous "rose leaf" sword in the Kunsthistorisches Museum in Vienna, and one in the Wallace Collection in London (no. A 477, old no. 49).

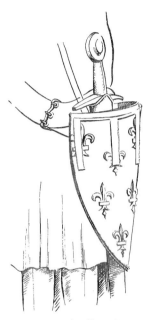

Fig. 28. Tomb effigy of Count Robert d'Artois, +1317, St. Denis.

CHAPTER TWO

Swords of Group II (1350–1550)

I N dealing with these swords we shall find that the chronology is more complicated, for most of the types from XV to XX were in use at various periods—or by their frequency in works of art appear to have been popular at various periods—throughout the whole of the two centuries between 1350–1550. There was a good deal of overlapping among the preceding types, but it is more noticeable with the later ones. The classification into sub-types, too, becomes more necessary, for in many of these swords the blade length might be constant but the grip-length varied, according, we may assume, to personal taste, as did the blade-section.

This will immediately be apparent in the next type.

TYPE XV CHARACTERISTICS

A strongly tapering, acutely pointed *blade* of four-sided "flattened diamond" section. The edges are straight, and taper without noticeable curves to the point, which may be strongly reinforced. The blade may be broad at the hilt (some 2″–2¼″) or quite narrow (about 1¼″). The *grip* is of medium length (about 4″) the *tang* generally narrow, of stout rectangular section, tapering a little towards the pommel. The *pommel* may be of any type, though variants of the disc or wheel forms predominate, except in the later examples of the period 1490–1520. The *cross* also may be of any style. In the earlier examples, *c.* 1280–1400, a cross of Style 8 is more usual—straight, with sharply downturned tips.

Type XV

General Remarks

At last we come to a sword type of which there are surviving examples to which we can put a date, though we must still rely upon art and literature for information as to the time of its earliest use. The episode related by Joinville which was included in the last chapter goes on to say how he got free of the Saracen's lance, wheeled his horse and tucking his sword (which, you will remember, he had drawn from its place in front of his saddle) under his arm "and using it in the manner of a lance", he ran upon his opponent and slew him. His sword must have had a pretty sharp point. Also mentioned was the sword shown on the monument in Salisbury Cathedral of William Longespée the Younger, who was himself killed in this battle of Mansourah; this (fig. 29) shows a blade with a

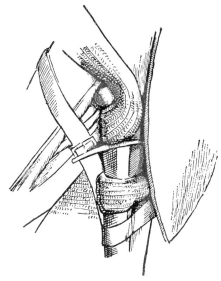

Fig. 29. Effigy of William Longespée the Younger, c. 1280. Salisbury Cathedral.

four-sided, mid-ribbed section. The monument dates about 1275–1290. A similar sword is on the splendid alabaster monument in Westminster Abbey to John of Eltham ($+$1337),[1] also shown as partly drawn from its scabbard so that the four-sided section can be seen. The "Romance of Alexander" of *c.* 1330 (also referred to in the last chapter) shows swords of Type XV.

This kind of sword is often depicted during the 14th century, and in Italian painting of the 15th it is extremely prevalent during the years 1420–1460. Piero della Francesca seems to have had a great liking for the type as so many examples are shown in his paintings. Uccello, on the other hand, favoured swords which appear to be of Type XVIIIa. It is most interesting to compare the great battle-pictures of the two contemporaries: the four panels of "The Rout of San Romano" of Uccello, and "The victory of Heraclius over Chosroes" in the church of St. Francis at Arezzo by Della Francesca. Pisanello's swords also tend to be of Type XVIII, while Luca Signorelli, at the end of the century, shows very clearly both XV's and XIX's.

These swords of Type XV did not seem to find favour in Germany. We rarely see them in 14th–15th century German art,

[1] Stothard, *Monumental Effigies.*

and few (if any) survivors are of a German character. It might be reasonable to say that the type was favoured (along with XIV's) in Western and Southern Europe during its early years between 1270 and 1370, and in Italy during the 15th century.

One of the most splendid survivors of the type is uncompromisingly Italian (plates 21 and 22B).[2] It was found in a grave in the Basilica of Monza, in or before 1698, with the body of a man naturally mummified by the quality of the soil. This body can be identified as that of Estore Visconti, who died on January 17th, 1413 as a result of a serious leg wound during a siege of Monza. This wound can still be seen on the left leg of the body. Identification is reinforced by the sword itself, which until recently bore upon the hilt the initials H.V. (for Hestor Viscomes). Inset into the pommel are four little silver shields, two bearing the arms of Visconti and two the arms of Milan. Estore was Lord of Milan jointly with his nephew Giovanni Carlo from May 1412 until he was driven out of the city a few weeks later. He retired to the castle of Monza where he was killed in 1413. So this sword cannot be later than 1413, and may have been made in 1412 or that year. However, it would be the easiest thing in the world to remove a little silver shield, set into a hollowed-out space in a pommel, and substitute another. The possibility that a new sword was made, bearing the arms of Visconti and of Milan, in those few weeks of 1412 when Estore held the lordship, is not nearly so strong as that a new shield was put on to it. Even so, here is a splendid Type XV sword datable before 1413. Many similar swords appear on monuments (mostly English) of the late 14th–early 15th centuries.[3]

Fig. 30. Blade sections.

Survivors of the earlier XV's are plentiful, but undatable. A fine, well-preserved sword in the Wallace Collection in London[4] (plate 22A) is typical, and by its hilt-form may well date

[2] Z.H.W.K. Blair, Claude, "The Sword of Estore Visconti". Vol IV, pl. 2. 1962.

[3] e.g. the brass of Sir Thomas Braunstone, Wisbech, Cambs.

[4] Wallace Collection no. A462 (old no. 5); Bruhn Hoffmeyer, pl. XXVa, p. 26. An identical sword is shown on the alabaster effigy, *c.* 1300, of Sir John de Hanbury, at Hanbury, Staffs.

before 1300. A very similar (nearly identical) one is in the collection of Mr. E. A. Christensen, though its blade is not as broad.[5]

During the second quarter of the 15th century (perhaps earlier) a new blade section appears. The four faces of the blade, instead of being flat or very gently hollowed, are so strongly hollowed out that a nearly flat blade with a powerful upstanding mid-rib results (fig. 30). It is impossible to say when this kind of blade came into use; surviving examples seem not to date earlier than 1425, though it is only a purely arbitrary dating; some—for example another sword in Mr. Christensen's collection[6]—could by their hilt forms be as early as 1380 or '90. Art does not help, for the actual hollowness of a blade's face is not easily shown. However, this blade-section is more often to be found on swords which are clearly of middle or late 15th century date.

The distinction between Types XV and XVa is clear, but there are many swords which seem to come midway between.

SUB-TYPE XVA CHARACTERISTICS

The *blade* is similar, though generally narrow and slender. The *grip* is much longer, from 7″ to 9″ or even 10″. Forms of *pommel* and *cross* are the same as for Type XV.

General Remarks

There are more surviving swords of this than of the type itself. Those which have always been held to be earliest in date (*c.* 1350–1380) are a group exemplified by one in the collection of the late Sir James Mann. This one was found in Northern France:[7] another was found in Lake Constance[8] (plate 27C), another two in the Thames in London,[9] another in Yorkshire,[10] and yet another has an Arabic inscription and probably came from Italy.[11] They vary a little in size, otherwise they seem almost identical. There are

Type XVa

[5] Coll. E. A. Christensen, Copenhagen; Bruhn Hoffmeyer, pl. XXIXa, p. 25.

[6] ibid., pl. XXIXb, p. 25.

[7] Formerly in the collection of the Baron C. A. de Cosson. Laking, op. cit., Vol. I, p. 140, fig. 175.

[8] In the collection of Sir Edward Barry, Bart. Laking, op. cit., Vol. I, p. 140, fig. 172.

[9] Collection of Society of Antiquaries. Laking, op. cit., Vol. I, p. 140, fig. 173, and a recent find (1959) in the Guildhall Museum in London.

[10] Victoria and Albert Museum, London.

[11] Collection of Mr. C. O. von Kienbusch, New York. Catalogue: the Kretzchmar von Kienbusch Collection. Princeton University, 1963, no. 326.

many others with slightly different hilts—one in the collection of Mr. J. Pocock (plate 14C) has a simple cross which is identical with that on the effigy of the Black Prince in Canterbury Cathedral.[12] A sword with exactly the same form and size of hilt, but a short blade, is in Berne.[13]

In the Tower of London is another (with a "scent-stopper" pommel) of Type XVa; this is particularly interesting as it has, just below the hilt, a piece about 6" long where the edges are thickened and squared off, forming a long "ricasso". The purpose of this was to enable the wielder to bring his left hand forward to grasp the sword below the cross, so that he could make a powerful two-handed thrust with a shortened blade in close fighting.[14]

These swords are of the well-known "Bastard" or "hand-and-a-half" kind. Eight out of ten military effigies and brasses of the period 1360–1420 show swords like this; there is only a limited variety in the forms of hilt, and the blades are long and slender. However, we cannot say for certain that they are of Type XVa, because they are sheathed; and many of the swords of Type XVII are of the same shape and proportions, but have a different blade-section.

There are many swords with blades of the right shape for the type but whose hilts are a little long to be of a true Type XV, and rather short for a XVa; for instance a particularly lovely sword (plate 24) in the Metropolitan Museum of Art in New York.[15] Such swords are typical of weapons which do not have the absolutely classic proportions of either type or sub-type, but which nevertheless must, because of the shape of their blades, be classed as of Type XV.

Type XV may seem to have been misplaced, for it continued in use for almost two centuries and was most popular after 1350, yet the sub-type seems to have gone completely out of use after about 1360. The reason is because it seems that Type XV began during the latter part of the 13th century, whereas XVI, on evidence at present available, may not have come into use until just after 1300.

---

[12] Stothard, op. cit.

[13] Bernische Historische Museum. Ms. No. 840. 1.

[14] Found near London Bridge in the Thames. Illustrated in *Arms and Armour in England*, Mann, Sir James, London, 1960, pl. 4e.

[15] Mu. No. 42. 50. 3. Bruhn Hoffmeyer, pl. XXVIIId, p. 31.

A strongly tapering *blade* of medium length (28″–32″); the upper half is broad, of a strong section with a well-marked, deep *fuller* which extends a little over half the length of the blade; the lower half tapers to an acute point, and is of stiff, solid four-sided "flattened diamond" section. The *grip* is of average length (about 4″); the *tang* is stout, often with the fuller running up into it. The hilt may be of any form. Many have variants of the "wheel" *pommel* but some have a type which has not hitherto appeared, in the form of a truncated wedge. The *cross* may also be of any style.

General Remarks

The most striking thing about these blades is that they seem very clearly to be made to serve the dual purpose of cutting and thrusting. The upper part of the blade is in the old style, while the lower part is acute enough, and stiff enough to thrust effectively. Thus it may have been equally useful against the armour prevalent in the first half of the 14th century—mail, mixed mail and plate (or "splinted armour"), or complete plate. While the point is acute enough even to penetrate plate armour,[16] there was enough width and edge at the "centre of percussion" or "optimal striking point"[17] to enable the blade to strike a very powerful shearing blow.

This is of course pure theorising, based upon the apparent practical features of the blade form. One of these swords is illustrated in plate 20B, and a glance at it will show that the

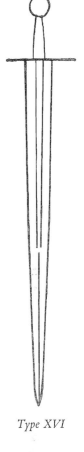

Type XVI

---

[16] Froissart describes at least two instances of sword-thrusts penetrating plate armour. Writing on an incident during the pursuit after the battle of Poitiers (1356) he says: "When the Lord of Berkeley had followed for some time, John de Hellenes turned about, put his sword under his arm in the manner of a lance, and thus advanced upon his adversary who, taking his sword by the handle, flourished it, and lifted up his arm to strike the squire as he passed. John de Hellenes, seeing the intended stroke, avoided it, but did not miss his own. For as they passed each other, by a blow on the arm he made Lord Berkeley's sword fall to the ground. When the knight found that he had lost his sword, and that the squire retained his own, he dismounted and made for the place where his sword lay. But before he could get there the squire gave him a violent thrust, which passed through both of his thighs so that he fell to the ground."

[17] A point at which, when the edge of the blade meets the object struck, there will be the least vibration of the blade, and where there is the most effective weight. This point varies according to the balance of the sword.

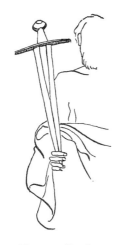

Fig. 31. St. Peter. Roof-boss in Exeter Cathedral, 1308–1328. Sword of Type XVI.

theory is feasible, and practical experience of doing these things with a blade like this proves that it is possible; we may assume they were designed and intended to cut through mail and pierce plate. We may reasonably date the type to the period when all those kinds of armour, previously mentioned, were in use together.

Luckily we need not rely upon theories. This dating is amply corroborated by works of art; there are many excellent representations of the type. One of the best is on an English roof-boss in Exeter Cathedral, in that part which can be dated between 1301 and 1338 (fig. 31). Others appear in "The Romance of Alexander" previously mentioned. Several are shown in German sculpture of c. 1300–1350,[18] others in French and Italian sculpture of the same period.

Fig. 33a. Mark on Type XVI sword in Lincoln.

Fig. 33b. Mark on Type XVI sword in Berne.

Fig. 32. Inscription on Type XVI blade in Copenhagen.

Actual survivors are not very plentiful; three excellent ones are in England,[19] another is in Denmark[20] (plate 20B), another (of a form identical to the Danish one, only with a longer blade) is in Berne.[21]

The one in Copenhagen has the letters +NINDIC+ inlaid in latten (fig. 32) in the fuller, an inscription of a style which seems to belong to the period 1300–1330.[22] The Berne specimen has a latten-inlaid mark (fig. 33b) which is of a character so similar to marks on two Type XVI blades in Lincoln (fig. 33a), which are generally held to be of early 14th century date, that it suggests the

[18] For instance, in the hand of St. Catherine on the tomb of Archbishop Mattheus von Bücheck (+1328) in Mainz Cathedral (fig. 46).

[19] In the Armouries of the Tower of London, in the London Museum (B. 306), and in the collection of Mr. J. C. Pocock, who has two.

[20] National Museum, Copenhagen, Inv. no. 16163. Bruhn Hoffmeyer, pl. XXXIIc, p. 34.

[21] Bernische Historische Museum, Inv. no. 840. 6.

[22] Wegeli, op. cit.

same workshop. It seems that the archaeological evidence coincides quite closely with the evidence of art in showing the type to be in use between 1300 and 1350—though, of course, there is no reason why individual swords may not still have been in use a century later; but if they were, they were probably a century old.

Like some of the preceding types, there is a sub-type to XVI which is in many ways more important than the type itself; there are several survivors.

SUB-TYPE XVIA CHARACTERISTICS

A long tapering *blade*, broad at the hilt, with a sharp point often strongly reinforced. The fuller is well-marked, often quite short (about $\frac{1}{3}$ of the blade's length) rarely more than half the length. The lower part of the blade is not of diamond section, but of a stout, flat hexagonal section. The *grip* is long, as in Types XIIIa and XVa, the *tang* of stout rectangular section, often with the fuller running up into it. The *pommel* may be of any type, but the commonest of surviving examples is the broad, flat wheel pommel of Type K, or another variant hitherto not found, a flat, oval form (Type H1).

General Remarks

These swords are generally said to belong to the late 14th–

Type XVIa

early 15th centuries, but the evidence does not uphold this. It might be said that Type XVIa is merely another variety of Type XIIIa, but it does seem, on the whole, to be a development of it, though undoubtedly in use at the same time. The acute points, often reinforced, suggest that it was opposed to plate or mixed armour. Hilt-forms, of course, tell us nothing about date. On all surviving specimens of the type, the hilts could equally well be of *c.* 1300 or *c.* 1450. Archaeological evidence that the type was in use quite early comes from a fine example found in the tomb of Albert I of Austria in the Cathedral of

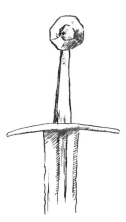

Fig. 34. Sword from the tomb of the Emperor Albrecht I, +1308, Spier Cathedral.

Spier (+1308).[23] Here the hilt is not very long, not truly of the "hand-and-a-half" kind, but it is longer than on many XVI's (fig. 34), and the blade is clearly representative of the type. A very similar weapon with an identical blade is in Copenhagen. This one has a mark stamped in the fuller below the cross (fig. 35) of a character very similar to several on the blades of swords of Type XIIIa.[24] This sword is dated by Ada Bruhn Hoffmeyer at *c.* 1250–1300,[25] but I believe it should be a little later, say *c.* 1290–1340. It is

Fig. 35. Mark on blade of Type XVIa sword in Copenhagen.

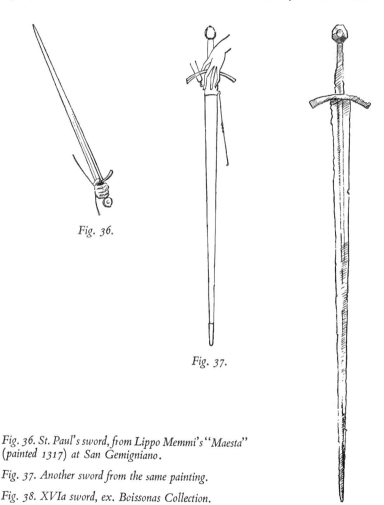

Fig. 36.

Fig. 37.

Fig. 36. St. Paul's sword, from Lippo Memmi's "Maesta" (painted 1317) at San Gemigniano.

Fig. 37. Another sword from the same painting.

Fig. 38. XVIa sword, ex. Boissonas Collection.

Fig. 38.

[23] Z.H.W.K. VII, 12, p. 257–360.

[24] Z.H.W.K. VIII, 8. The same mark occurs on the Thorpe Falchion (Norwich Museum), plate 26B.

[25] Bruhn Hoffmeyer, pl. XIVf, p. 16.

not, I am sure, as late as 1380–1400. Another very fine example indeed is in the Armouries of the Tower of London[26] (plate 29). This has been thought to date in the early 15th century, surely 100 years too late. It has one of those Arabic inscriptions just below the hilt (unfortunately one which gives no date)[27] but, as we have seen in the case of the Type XIIIb swords in the Kienbusch and Christensen collections, the sword may have been—most probably was—made many decades before the inscription was added.

There are many of these swords, nearly all once thought to be of the late 14th or early 15th centuries. The earlier dating which I suggest is well supported by a number of clearly shown swords in Italian paintings of the early 14th century. A St. Paul in a "Maesta" by Lippo Memmi, painted in 1317 and now in the Town Hall of San Gimigniano, shows one very clearly (fig. 36), for the blade is bare. An identical one in the same picture is sheathed (fig. 37). Another St. Paul by Signa di Bonaventura of the same period (Accademia, Siena) shows another. A fourth is in a painting (c. 1330) by Barna di Siena in the Ehrich Gallery, New York. The naked sword in Lippo Memmi's "Maesta" is paralleled by an absolutely identical weapon once in the Boissonas Collection (fig. 38),[28] whose blade, however, seems to be of a very long and attenuated Type XVI.

TYPE XVII CHARACTERISTICS

A long, slender *blade* acutely tapering. Many are reminiscent of 16th century rapier blades, but others are nearly as broad at the hilt ($1\frac{1}{2}''$–$2''$) as some of the XVIa blades. The section is generally hexagonal. Many examples have a shallow *fuller* in the upper quarter of the blade, though some do not. The *grip* is always long. The *tang* usually very stout, of a quadrangular section. The *pommel* is either of a flattened oval shape (Type H1) or of one of the "scent-stopper" forms (Types T, T2, or T4) which first appeared late in the 14th century. The *cross* may be of any style, though 1a and 6 seem to have been most popular.

Type XVII

General Remarks

This is a sword-type which offers no complications. There are

---

[26] No. IX. 915.

[27] It merely says "Inalienable property of the Treasury of the Marsh province of Alexandria. May it be protected".

[28] *Armes Anciennes de la Suisse*, plate X, 5.

some clearly datable examples, and English monuments between *c.* 1355 and 1425 show them almost exclusively—with the reservation that the swords are shown sheathed, and so might be of Type XVa. It is essentially a thrusting sword, some being more like stout, sharp-pointed bars of steel. They are much heavier than the earlier types; an ordinary XVII may weigh as much as $5\frac{1}{2}$ lbs. as against $3\frac{1}{2}$ lbs. to 4 lbs. of a XIIIa. This great weight would make the weapon effective to some extent as a cracker of plate armour. It is significant that in this period (1360–1420) when complete plate armour was at its most solid (before the musket-proof attempts of the 16th century) that the favourite knightly weapons were the axe, mace and war hammer. The swords of Type XVII seem to have been designed to compete with these smashing weapons.

The best datable examples are two swords found in the Abbey of Königsfeld, Aarau, Switzerland, in the graves of two of the Austrian knights who fell in 1386 in the battle of Sempach, Frederiks von Tarant and Friedrich von Griffenstein.[29] These swords are of the classic Type XVII with scent-stopper pommels of Type T2. A sword almost identical with von Tarant's is in the Fitzwilliam Museum in Cambridge, perhaps one of the most graceful swords to survive to the present day.[30] In its blade is

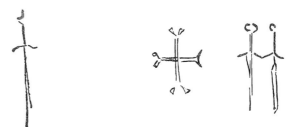

Fig. 39. Mark on "The Redfern Sword", Fitzwilliam Museum, Cambridge.

Fig. 40. Marks on the sword of Frederiks von Tarant, killed at Sempach in 1386.

inlaid a mark (fig. 39), a little, rather spindly-looking sword very different from those in the blades of the Guildhall and Gwynn examples of XIIIa (p. 48, fig. 22). An almost identical mark is on the von Tarant sword (fig. 40), except that there are two swords side by side. Another sword of this type, very nearly as perfect as

[29] Z.H.W.K. VI, 6, p. 204. In the Kantonales Antiquarium, Aarau.

[30] Once in the Redfern collection, and world famous as "The Redfern Sword", published and illustrated in Laking, op. cit., vol. II, p. 254, fig. 630.

the Cambridge one though somewhat smaller, is in the collection of Mr. R. T. Gwynn. There are so many of these swords that it would be impossible to mention more than a few, but two in the collection of Mr. E. A. Christensen are of the other classic form of the type with oval pommels of Type H1. One of these (plate 30B) is the best preserved of them all, and has a long Arabic inscription giving the date 1427.[31]

A very large example, found in the Thames in Sion Reach, near Kew, is in the London Museum. This has almost the proportions of a "Twahandswerd" 54·4″ overall.[32] In the same museum there is a blade with a part of its hilt, also found in London, which is extremely similar to the Sion Reach one but is a few inches shorter.[33] A sword of similar shape and dimensions only of superlative quality is the "Pearl" sword of the City of Bristol. This was given to the city as a sword of ceremony by Sir John de Wells in 1431, a date valuable in placing the style of the beautiful silver gilt hilt (see chap. 3, p. 109).

Another Type XVII sword of superlative quality (plate 30C), is in the Bayerisches National Museum at Munich.[34]

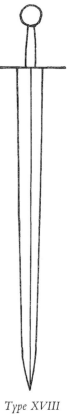

Type XVIII

TYPE XVIII CHARACTERISTICS

A broad *blade* ($2″$–$2\frac{1}{2}″$ at the hilt) of four-sided "flattened diamond" section; the edges taper in graceful curves to a sharp point. The *grip* is of moderate length ($3\frac{3}{4}″$–$4″$) but some are big swords with grips over $5″$ long. A feature of the grips of these swords—many are preserved—is a noticeable swelling in the middle (as plate 46D, fig. 75, p. 104). The *pommel* may be of one of the varieties of wheel-pommel (generally types I, J or J1) or of one of the "scent-stopper" forms (Type T, T3, or T5, or of Type V). The *cross* is generally curved, and in many examples is of style 11.

[31] Vaabenshistoriske Aarboge, vol. VIIa; Bruhn Hoffmeyer, Ada, "To Ridderswerd i en Dansk Privatsammling".
[32] London Museum No. 39.142. Illustrated in Mediaeval Catalogue, p. 36, fig. 6; and Laking, op. cit., vol. II, p. 252, fig. 627. Formerly in the Henry C. Keasby collection.
[33] London Museum No. A 2453. Mediaeval Catalogue, p. 35, fig. 4, and plate III.
[34] The blade bears an interesting inscription. Z.H.W.K. Wegeli, op. cit.

General Remarks

This type is very hard to distinguish from Type XV. The difference, however, is clear, though subtle. In XV, the edges run quite straight to the acute point, giving a very narrow appearance to the lower part of the blade. In XVIII, the edges run in curves, and the lower part of the blade looks broader. The type is, in fact, admirably adapted for a cut-and-thrust style of fighting, and seems to be a logical development of Type XVI. The strong mid-rib gives great rigidity, yet toward the point at the centre of percussion there is plenty of width to each edge. The section varies, the four faces may be quite flat, but more usually they are gently hollowed; in later examples the sharp upstanding rib rising from a flat blade is found (fig. 105). Some XVIII's which have been much used and often sharpened are impossible to distinguish from XV's; a good example is a sword in the Wallace Collection in London (no. A.460, old no. 8, plate 35A).

This type, and its four sub-types, were the most widely used swords between c. 1410 and 1510 all over Europe. It may well have been in use in the late 14th century, but the earliest date we so far have for it is 1419; this is inscribed in Arabic on a very fine sword of the type in the Metropolitan Museum in New York.[35]

Another to which we can with some confidence give a terminating date of 1422 is a lovely little sword preserved in Westminster Abbey, a very well-known weapon which may with reasonable certainty be said to have been deposited in the Abbey after the funeral of Henry V.[36] After this there are several datable examples, mostly swords once belonging to members of the royal houses of Germany. That the type of the Henry V swords was still used at the very end of the century is proved by a magnificent sword (plate 35B) in the Kunsthistorisches Museum in Vienna,[37] a ceremonial sword (but not, as so many were, of outsize proportions) made, possibly for Philip the Handsome, in Milan about 1490. Examples of the blade-form, almost indis-

---

[35] Metropolitan Museum no. 29,150,143. Bruhn Hoffmeyer, vol. II, pl. XXVIIIa, p. 31.

[36] *Antiquaries Journal*, Mann, J. G., The Connoisseur, 1950. Oakeshott, R. Ewart, "A 'Royal' sword preserved in the Library of Westminster Abbey". Laking, op. cit. vol. II, p. 262, fig. 640.

[37] Kunsthistorische Museum, Vienna, Inv. no. A 456 W. Published in the "Jahrbuch" Band 57, 1951, fig. 22.

tinguishable from those of the 15th century, continued to be popular until the 18th.

A feature quite often found in the blades of Type XVIII (but more frequently in sub-type XVIIIa) is a built-up shoulder to the blade, almost an incipient ricasso. Though not unknown on blades of the 12th, 13th and 14th centuries,[38] this feature had been rare since the Roman Iron Age.[39] As the 15th century progressed it became more common, until by its end few blades of this form were without it. (The development of the ricasso itself will be dealt with under Type XIX.)

SUB-TYPE XVIIIA CHARACTERISTICS

A fairly slender *blade*, average length about 32″. The section the same as XVIII, but some have a narrow fuller in the upper part. A single-handed type, but some are big weapons with quite long grips (about 5″). *Pommel* and *cross* may be of any type of style.

General Remarks

There are perhaps more survivors of this than of the type itself, for there is one in practically every collection; and many are among the most beautiful weapons ever made (plates 36A and 43B) for they combine grace of line and purity of form with the utmost practical effectiveness. Examples show almost every kind of hilt used during the 15th century, from the classic forms of the 13th century to all the new varieties of pommel and cross which developed after 1400. These hilt-forms, and the swords they adorn, will be dealt with in their proper place. Here words are unnecessary; the sub-type has been illustrated quite fully, and the photographs speak more usefully than any attempt at description.

There are a few datable examples, but now that the types are all within the 15th century, most individual swords can be dated, even to within a decade, by the fashion of their hilts and by the representation of similar ones in datable works of art. It is also possible now to say that a given sword may be German or Italian; Spanish swords of the 15th century are even easier to

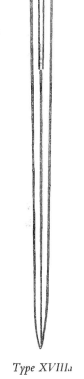

Type XVIIIa

[38] For instance, a sword of *c.* 1150 in the collection of Mr. Harold Peterson, Arlington, Virginia; one (op. cit., p. 50) in my own collection; another in the Armouries of the Tower of London (op. cit., p. 62, note 19).
[39] Engelhardt, "Vimosefundet"; Davidson, op. cit.

69

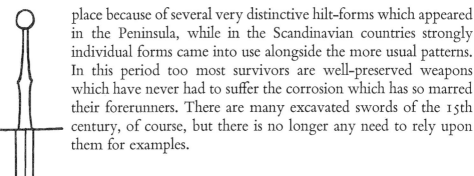

place because of several very distinctive hilt-forms which appeared in the Peninsula, while in the Scandinavian countries strongly individual forms came into use alongside the more usual patterns. In this period too most survivors are well-preserved weapons which have never had to suffer the corrosion which has so marred their forerunners. There are many excavated swords of the 15th century, of course, but there is no longer any need to rely upon them for examples.

SUB-TYPE XVIIIB CHARACTERISTICS

A long, slender, acutely pointed *blade*, generally of "flattened diamond" section, often with the point reinforced. The *grip* is very long, often as much as 10″–11″. The *pommel* is most frequently of one of the wheel forms, but second to those in popularity seem to have been the scent-stopper and fruit shaped ones of Types T and T5. *Crosses* are generally long and slender, more often straight than curved. The *grip* is of a very characteristic shape, with a waisted lower half which merges with a slender upper half.

General Remarks

There are many of these swords, particularly in German collections, and many are to be seen in art, particularly German paintings of the period 1450–1520. Dürer shows many examples which are well-known.[40] The finest survivor of the type—indeed, perhaps the most lovely sword of any period or place—is in the Bayerische National Museum at Munich[41] (plates 33B and 45). Not only has this sword absolute perfection of line and proportion, but its preservation is perfect, and the decoration of grip, pommel and cross is restrained and beautiful, admirably suited to the hilt it adorns. One may unhesitatingly say that here is the very epitome of a "hand-and-a-half" sword of the second half of the 15th century, a German one exactly similar to so many carried by Dürer's saints and knights. Its hilt has often been illustrated, but rarely the whole sword—a great pity, since the hilt alone gives no idea of the absolute splendour of it.

A very well-preserved though plain sword of this type, dating

Type XVIIIb

[40] For instance: "This is the manner of arming at the present time", dated 1494; "The Vision of St. Hubert"; "The Knight, Death and the Devil", and many others.
[41] Bayerische National Museum, Inv. no. W. 872. Bruhn Hoffmeyer, vol. II, pl. XXIIa, p. 22.

perhaps a little earlier than the one just mentioned, used to be in the De Cosson Collection, and was sold at Sotheby's in 1946.[42] It is now in the United States, presumably in a private collection since it cannot be traced. A remarkably similar sword is shown in an Italian painting of *c.* 1474, a Coronation of the Virgin by Giovanni Bellini in the Gallery at Pesaro (fig. 41). Another,[43] sold from the same collection as the first (illustrated alongside it in the sale catalogue), has a rather unusual blade. It may, with some stretching of the imagination, be placed in sub-type XVIIIb, but the blade's edges run very nearly parallel to end in a cut, rather angular, point, giving it a clumsy appearance. This sword too is lost sight of.

SUB-TYPE XVIIIC CHARACTERISTICS

A broad, heavy *blade*, of "flattened diamond" section, the faces nearly always flat or slightly convex, generally about 34″ long. The *grip* is long, rather like those grips of some type XVIII swords with a sharp swelling in the middle. As these big swords are hand-and-a-half weapons, the swelling is nearer to the cross than to the pommel.

Fig. 41. From a "Coronation of the Virgin" by Giovanni Bellini, c. 1474, Pesaro.

The *pommel* is generally of one of the wheel forms. The *cross* is often of flat ribbon-like section (style 5) but horizontally curved into a flat S shape.

General Remarks

This seems to be a characteristically Italian style of the type, corresponding to the German XVIIIb. Survivors are rare. There

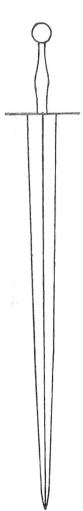

Type XVIIIc

---

[42] De Cosson sale, May 23rd, 1946, Sotheby's. Catalogue lot 147.
[43] ibid. lot 144.

is a fine one in the Metropolitan Museum in New York,[44] and a very similar one in my own collection.

SUB-TYPE XVIIID CHARACTERISTICS

A long, slender *blade*, of stiff four-sided section, sometimes with a deep and narrow *fuller* running the whole length. Short *grip*. The *pommel* is generally of one of the wheel forms, the *cross* often horizontally curved, but in some cases very sharply curved downwards. Some of these swords have the hilt with "pas d'âne" and side rings which developed (? in Spain) during the second half of the 15th century.

General Remarks

These swords seem to be rather a heterogeneous lot; it is possible to classify most as of a sub-type to type XVIII, but a few are more or less unplaceable. Good examples are (1) in the Wallace Collection (no. A467, old no. 46) with a wheel pommel of type J1 and a horizontally curved cross; (2) in the Armouries of the Tower of London with a pear-shaped pommel and a sharply down-turned cross,[45] and (3) one in my own collection with a developed hilt (plate 38).[46]

SUB-TYPE XVIIIE CHARACTERISTICS

A long, narrow *blade* generally with a long (5"–6") ricasso narrower than the blade itself; occasionally with a *fuller* running most of the length, but more commonly of "flattened diamond" section. *Pommel* of pear form, and the *cross* is curved sharply downward.

Type XVIIId

General Remarks

So many of these swords have been found in Denmark (including one which belonged to King Christian I, 1450–1481)[47] that it may be said that they are a characteristically Danish type. Even so, others may be of Italian origin. A particularly fine one

---

[44] Metropolitan Museum, Inv. no. 26. 259. 2. Bruhn Hoffmeyer, vol. II, pl. XXIIc, p. 24.·

[45] Armouries, Tower of London. Formerly in the Norton Hall Collection.

[46] Blair, Claude, *European and American Arms*, Batsford, 1962.

[47] Roskilde Cathedral, Chapel of Christian I; Bruhn Hoffmeyer, vol. II, pl. XXXVIc, p. 41.

used to be in the De Cosson Collection, which might be Italian,[48] and another was in the Henry Keasby Collection; De Cosson and Laking[49] called this one Italian too, but though it has features (the pommel and cross shapes) which might be called Italian, they are also exactly like the large number found in Denmark. King Christian's sword might, by the same token, be called Italian. It does seem, on the whole, that sub-type XVIIIe is Danish.

Many of these have enormously long grips (fig. 42) bound at intervals with bands of metal.[50]

Fig. 42. XVIIIe sword, Danish type, Copenhagen.

TYPE XIX CHARACTERISTICS

Broad flat *blade*, the edges running nearly parallel to a sudden sharp point, with a narrow well-moulded *fuller* in the upper third. The section is a flat hexagon—i.e. the blade itself is flat, with the edges clearly chamfered, as in Type XVIa. There is a well-made ricasso, almost $2\frac{1}{2}''$–3″ long. As there are at the moment very few known examples of this type, one cannot say what form the average hilt takes. The *grip* however is quite short; it is a single-handed weapon.

General Remarks

This is a type of blade which until recently was not recognised as being used before the mid-16th century. Two of the swords of Type XIX, however, give clear dates. One, in the Armouries of the Tower of London (plate 39B)[51] has an Arabic inscription giving the date 1432. Thus it is clear that the sword must date before that.

The hilt of this sword is also of extreme interest, for it has a

Type XVIIIe

---

[48] Sotheby's, 1946. Lot 151.
[49] Laking, op. cit., vol. II, p. 257, fig. 634.
[50] Bruhn Hoffmeyer, vol. II, pl. XXXVe.
[51] Armouries, Tower of London, purchased from the collection of W. R. Hearst.

Type XIX

small single ring below the cross on one side (see chap. 4, pp. 118–19). A second sword of the type, in the Royal Ontario Museum in Toronto (plate 39A), also has an Arabic inscription giving the early date of 1368.[52] The hilt of this sword is of a type one might expect to find at that date—a flat, truncated wedge-shaped pommel with the corners rounded, and a cross of style 6, exactly like that on so many swords of this period. The Tower example has a similar cross, of Style 5, and a flat disc pommel. The blades of both swords are identical, bearing the same mark. A third, and little-known, sword of this type is in the Museum of Ethnology and Archaeology in Cambridge. Here the sword has been excavated and its outline is marred, but it seems to have tapered more acutely than the preceding examples. The ricasso is a little shorter. The hilt has a long pear-shaped pommel of Type T4 and a long cross of Style 5 horizontally curved to a flat S shape.[53]

I know of no positively identifiable examples of this type in art, but those two with Arabic inscriptions give us a firm terminating date; the fact that similar blades are to be found on 16th century swords as well as many of the late 15th is an indication that the type went on.

There are several late 15th century examples, with fully developed hilts with "pas d'ânes" and side-rings. Most are of Spanish origin—i.e. the sword of Gonsalvo de Cordova (1453–1515) in the Armeria Real at Madrid,[54] another in the same collection attributed to Ferdinand the Catholic,[55] another (plate 39C) in the collection of the Instituto del Conde de Valencia de Don Juan,[56] and another—a very small one, perhaps made for a boy—in the collection of the late Sir James Mann. Many swords of this kind (but sheathed, so we cannot say whether the blades are the same) are shown in the paintings of the Portuguese artist Nuño Gonçalves. These are important, since they have an early and positive date—*c.* 1460.

[52] Royal Ontario Museum, no. M.973, published in Combe and De Cosson, op. cit.
[53] Cambridge University, Museum of Ethnology and Archaeology.
[54] Madrid, Armeria Real, Inv. no. G.29. Catalogo Historico-Descriptivo de la Armeria Real de Madrid. El Conde de Valencia de Don Juan, Madrid, 1878.
[55] ibid, no. G.31.
[56] Instituto del Conde de Valencia de Don Juan.

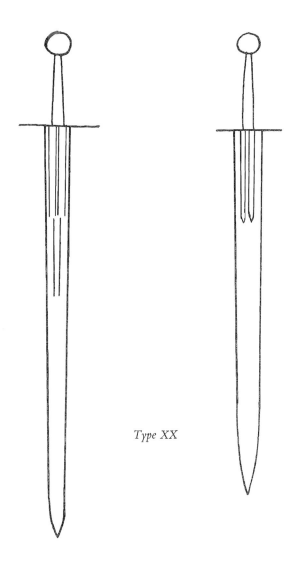

Type XX

TYPE XX CHARACTERISTICS

A large, broad *blade* sometimes extremely wide at the hilt. Many examples have three shallow fullers in the upper half, two side by side immediately below the hilt, and a single one in the middle of the blade below them. Others may have two very narrow, deep fullers side by side extending about a quarter of the blade length. *Hilts* are usually long (about 8″–10″) with scent-stopper *pommels* of Type T. Some may have wheel pommels. *Crosses* are generally long and slender, curved slightly—or rather, each arm inclines at an angle downward, but remains straight (plate 40).

General Remarks

Some of these swords are war-swords, a sort of late development of Type XIIIa, in use at the same time as the late examples
of that type. Such are two swords (plate 40C and A), one in the
collection of Claude Blair[57] and the other in the Waffensammlung
in Vienna.[58] The first of these has an Arabic inscription; one of
those giving a clear date, in this case 1427. The second is not
dated, but by its general style might be placed in the middle years
of the 15th century; yet because of its similarity to a very large
"bearing sword" of identical form in the collection of Mr. R. T.
Gwynn of Epsom (plate 40B) which has recently been dated
within the first quarter of the 14th century, the sword in Vienna
must be of a roughly similar date. A rather similar but even larger
one is in the Victoria and Albert Museum in London.[59]

An extremely handsome sword of Type XX is in the Dresden
Ruskammer, the sword of Frederic of Saxony which can be dated
at *c.* 1424–5. This is a sword of ceremony, not a fighting weapon,
but none the less a good example of the type.[60]

A most splendid example of the other form of Type XX is
another ceremonial sword, made for Frederic, King of the
Romans from 1440 to 1453, afterwards the Emperor Frederic
III (plate 42A).

SUB-TYPE XXA CHARACTERISTICS

A broad *blade*, tapering rather more sharply than in Type XX
but with the same arrangement of fullering. A one-hand weapon,
with a short grip. The *pommel* is always of one of the varieties of
the wheel or disc forms, and the *cross* is always short and very
sharply arched, though some have hilts of cinquedea form.

Type XXa   ### General Remarks

There are not many of these swords, but most of the survivors
are extremely rich and splendid weapons. At the head of them is

---

[57] Blair, Claude, *European and American Weapons*, and Journal of the Arms and
Armour Society, 1959.

[58] Kunsthistorisches Museum, Vienna, inv. no. A.89. W.

[59] This is probably of late date—*c.* 1550–80.

[60] Haenel, E., *Kostbare Waffen*, Dresden, 1928, pl. 80, and Bruhn Hoffmeyer,
vol. II, pl. XXVIa. Also Thomas, B., Gamber, O., and Schedelmann, H., *Die
Schönsten Waffen*.

the magnificent sword made in 1493 for Cesare Borgia.[61] This is a quite outstanding weapon, and although the exquisite decoration in copper-gilt and translucent enamels is of a purely Renaissance character, the sword itself has all the characteristic simplicity of the knightly weapon. A rather similar, though much plainer, weapon of this type used to be in the De Cosson Collection.[62] The hilt is of the same shape and proportions as the Borgia sword; the disc-shaped pommel encloses a medal struck to commemorate the Battle of the Garigiliano (perhaps the most notable victory of "The great Captain" Gonsalvo de Cordova) in 1503. There are unfortunately few of these very handsome swords, none in an English collection, unless one excepts a very small example (perhaps made for a boy) in my own (plate 44C). An early and dated specimen of the type is a beautiful sword, also of a cere-monial character, made c. 1435 for Sigismund, King of Hungary, later Emperor (plate 42B). This is in the Kunsthistorisches Museum in Vienna.

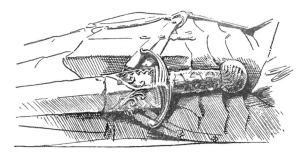

Fig. 43. Effigy of Sir Robert Harcourt, +1471.
Stanton Harcourt, Oxford.

We do not often find these swords in art. They are, in fact, of an almost local character, all being North Italian. There is one shown on an English effigy, that of Sir Robert Harcourt at Stanton Harcourt in Oxfordshire (fig. 43), and others which may be of the type on the brass of John Diggis, c. 1450, at Borham, Kent, and of Henry Mitchell, d. 1510, at Floore, Northants— another indication of the fashion for Italian armour and weapons in 15th century England.

[61] Coll. Duke of Sermoneta. Laking, op. cit., vol. II, p. 272, fig. 648, and pp. 270–77. Also E.-de Beaumont, Fleur des Belles Epées.

[62] Laking, op. cit., vol. II, p. 273, fig. 652. Catalogue, Sotheby's, 14th May, 1929, lot 98.

Fig. 44. Renaissance hilt on sword of Type XXa.

The other variety of this sub-type has a hilt in the style of the cinquedea. Some of these are rather ugly, a few outstandingly beautiful. In the Armouries of the Tower of London is a very fine one of excellent proportions. Another, which used to be in the De Cosson Collection and later in my own, is in the possession of Mr. David Drey in London (plate 44).[63] Another variety, similarly hilted but with a blade of the same shape as the sword of Frederic III, used to be in the Bashford Dean Collection in New York. Later it came into my possession, but was disposed of in an exchange and is now lost trace of (plate 42C).[64] Another of this kind is in the Armouries of the Tower of London.

Some swords which fall within Types XX or XXa have elaborately decorated hilts of purely Renaissance form, but must be regarded as late medieval (fig. 44). On the other hand, there are very many short swords dating between about 1490 and 1530 which, while they have affinities with Type XXa, are very varied and diverse and all of purely Renaissance form.

The cinquedea, on the other hand, might well be classified with this type; but it is a specialised weapon, hardly a sword and not a dagger, used mainly for show—if one may use a modern idiom—as a status symbol to be carried by a page before his master, resting in all its decorative glory upon a cushion.

The observant reader will find that there are many 15th century swords which do not fall neatly into any of the types here set out. Very occasionally this is for the same reason that so many do not seem to fit into the earlier type of the 12th and 13th centuries, i.e. because they are broken or corroded; but more often it is that during the last phase of the Middle Ages a great many strongly

[63] De Cosson Coll., Sotheby's, May 23rd, 1946, lot 139. *Archaeology of Weapons*, p. 339, pl. 9b. Catalogue, Victoria and Albert Museum, C.I.N.O.A. International Art Treasures Exhibition, Cat. 320, 419, pl. 227.
[64] Ex.-Coll. W. Bashford Dean, Douglas Ash, Ewart Oakeshott. It has since been sold by Fischer of Lucerne.

individual swords were made, some of eccentric form. There are a few, however, which might have been classified as a sub-type of XVIII. These are very rare—indeed, I only know of two examples, one which used until 1929 to be in the De Cosson Collection and another which is in the Armeria Real at Madrid. Both are hand-and-a-half swords, but are characterised by having small lugs projecting from each edge just below the ricasso. The De Cosson example (fig. 45) is a particularly handsome weapon, its grip and pommel of a form characteristic of

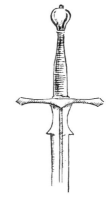

Fig. 45. *Sword of a type so far indefinable, ex. De Cosson Collection.*

the period 1410–1440.[65] Though a hand-and-a-half sword the grip is not very long, unlike the larger example in Madrid which, while having a similar blade, cross and pommel, has a much larger grip.[66] These two are ordinary swords, but there are many others dating between perhaps 1450–1525 which, while having the same characteristics, are two-handers—indeed, these are probably the direct forerunners of the typical and well-known two-hander of the 16th century. Most of these seem to be Spanish, and there are several in Madrid. They are given the name of "Montante".

Fig. 46. *Sword in the hand of a figure of St. Catherine, from the tomb in Mainz Cathedral of Mattheus von Bücheck, +1328. Type XVI.*
(See p. 62.)

[65] De Cosson, Sotheby's, May 14th, 1929, lot 96, pl. 1.
[66] ibid., lot 89, p. 1. Madrid, Armeria Real, no. G.15. Catalogue, fig. 113.

CHAPTER THREE

Pommel-Forms

D URING the later Middle Ages there was almost limitless variety in the forms of pommels and cross-guards. Considering the permutations which might result from the juxtaposition of these varied elements, the difficulties of classifying swords by these hilt-forms are obvious. However, pommels can be classified into 35 basic types, and cross-guards into 12 distinct styles. Individual variation upon any of these basic forms was decorative and so does not really affect the typology, but examples will always appear which defy classification, e.g. plate 46C.

Perhaps the most widely used pommel during the three centuries between *c.* 950 and *c.* 1250 is that which is generally known as the Brazil-nut form. It is perhaps also the most widely misunderstood, and the most often mis-dated. Therefore it may be expedient to begin with a detailed analysis of its development and image, treating it with a thoroughness not necessary in the case of other types.

It has been generally assumed that pommels of this form were in use during a period extending roughly from 1150 to 1250. There is, however, ample evidence—clearly datable iconographical evidence—to show that swords were furnished with them 200 years before this period, and that their use was general throughout the 11th and 12th centuries, particularly in Germany.

There are two other current misconceptions about the Brazil-nut pommel—that it developed from the so-called "Mushroom" form and eventually superseded it, and that the extent of the upward curvature of its lower edge is an indication of development and so of date. It has been stated by many authorities, in rather vague terms, that the Brazil-nut began to develop from the Mushroom form early in the 12th century, and that during the next 150 years the curvature of its base steadily grew until by about

1230 the upper edge was straight. The evidence shows conclusively that this was not so; both forms developed simultaneously in the early to middle 10th century, if not before; all the different varieties of the Brazil-nut, with a greater or lesser degree of curvature to their bases, were in use at the same time, alongside the more familiar lobated types of Viking pommel, and the variations in its shape were probably the result of chance or personal taste and not a matter of date at all.

Fig. 47. INGELRII *sword from the Danube at Hilgartsberg, Munich.*

Before going farther I should mention that this so-called Mushroom form of pommel is not a bit like a mushroom; in plan it is flat, not circular as a mushroom is. It would be much nearer the mark to liken it to a tea-cosy; the flatter ones to an empty tea-cosy, and those with more bulk to a tea-cosy with a teapot inside. The German antiquarians who described it as "Pilzformige" probably intended to liken it to certain kinds of toadstool; "mushroom" is too free a translation in this case, and I shall continue to refer to it here as "the Tea-Cosy pommel" (see p. 27 above, figs. 4 and 5).

This Tea-Cosy pommel seems to have had an earlier origin and a shorter term of popularity than its cousin of the Brazil-nut shape. We find occasional portrayals of it in sculpture, engraved work, and painting down to about 1160, though not frequently after 1100. The Brazil-nut pommel, on the other hand, continued in use for another 150 years. In the mid-12th century it began to develop a greater bulk, and in the later years of the same century several derivative forms appeared. The original shape of the 10th century was never quite lost, but the later types are easily recognisable by their much more massive appearance.

There is another pommel type which should be noted in connection with the Brazil-nut; it is generally (and aptly) called the "Hat" form, owing to its resemblance to a cocked hat. In its origin it was quite unlike the nut and Tea-Cosy types, for it was made in two parts and looked more like a simplification of the trilobate Viking types. It first seems to have appeared in the late

81

10th century, and in its final forms of the mid-13th it merged with the latest of the Brazil-nut forms.

The earliest datable swords with Tea-Cosy pommels were found in the Seine below Paris where there was so much fighting during the famous siege in 885-6.[1] The earliest Brazil-nut pommels have been found in Norwegian graves of about 950.[2] These types differed from all other pommels of the Viking age in that they were forged from one piece of iron, not an upper and lower piece bolted together; neither have they any incised lines or mouldings to simulate the separation of the two parts. Fig. 4 in chapter I shows one of these grave-finds, from Sandeherred in Norway; the lower edge is curved slightly upward, so it comes within the Brazil-nut group. Fig. 47 is a sword whose pommel is of a more distinctly nut-like shape. It was found in the Danube near Hilgartsberg and is now in Munich.[3] Inlaid in its blade in iron letters is the smith-name INGELRIÍ.

Another good sword with both INGELRIÍ blade and Brazil-nut pommel is in the Hanover State Museum;[4] in this case the pommel is short, rather like the sword from Sandeherred. Almost identical is an INGELRIÍ sword in my own collection (plate 1C).

There have been few of these swords among the Scandinavian finds, but many of both forms have been excavated in central and north-western Europe. Of these only a few were found in graves; the majority were dug from the earth or from the beds of rivers. A noticeable thing about the distribution of these finds is that most with the Tea-Cosy pommel have appeared in western or coastal regions, from the Baltic coast of Germany to the mouth of the Loire, while the greater number with the Brazil-nut pommel have been found in central or eastern Europe. This marked local separation of the two groups seems to suggest that the former were a type more popular with the "Colonial" Danes, as they are found in regions where the Vikings of the 10th century settled, or at least raided most frequently, while the latter were perhaps an indigenous Central European type used by the Germans and Austrasian Franks. It may be possible to classify these two forms of this pommel, classified by Petersen as

[1] e.g. Gay, op. cit., p. 642, fig. G, under "Epée".
[2] Petersen, op. cit., p. 166, fig. 129.
[3] Munich, Bayerische National Museum, Inv. no. IV, 873.
[4] Hanover, State Museum. Inv. no. 218:32.

the "X-type", under two regional groups as the Neustrian and Austrasian types, thus going one step farther than those authorities who have referred to the Tea-Cosy pommel as "the Norman type".

German manuscript illustration of the Ottonian period (roughly between about 950 and 1050) provides many clear and datable examples of the two types, though most are of the Austrasian or Brazil-nut form. Many of these manuscripts, particularly those made by the artists of Reichenau and St. Gall, contain extremely fine paintings of a high artistic quality; they show either formal portraits of emperors such as Otto III or Heinrich II or Biblical scenes of battles, massacres, martyrdoms, and murders wherein many swords appear. It may be thought that these paintings cannot be reliable as sources of information about small details such as sword-hilts, but before condemning them out of hand two things have to be taken into consideration. One is the well-established fact that the medieval artist was meticulous in accurately depicting objects in everyday use—this can be proved over and over again by comparing surviving specimens of such objects, sword-hilts included, with the pictures of them. The other is that the sword ranked so high in contemporary estimation that it is not likely to have been regarded as an unimportant detail and so treated summarily. Of course, there are some manuscript paintings which by contemporary standards are very bad, and so cannot be considered in this connection. It is very noticeable that in the best of these Ottonian paintings, and even more in German monumental sculpture of the High Middle Ages, swords seen in these works of art can be compared with actual surviving examples of the same date and type to show how closely the artist observed the original.

I have drawn upon a few of the best of these manuscripts for illustrations of the early "X-type" (my Type A) pommels. Perhaps the finest of all in this connection is the Dedication page from a manuscript made for the Emperor Otto III in Reichenau between the years 983 and 991.[5] It shows the emperor enthroned, supported by noblemen of his court, while the Four Nations do homage to him. The treatment is almost monumental in style, very restrained and dignified, and gives us a noble yet lively

[5] Formerly in the Cathedral Treasury at Bamberg, now in the Staatsbibliothek, Munich, Cod. Lat. 4453.

Fig. 48. From "The Gospels of Otto III".

portrait of the emperor. Scarcely less striking is the figure of the venerable nobleman standing at his left hand holding his sword. It will be seen how clearly and carefully this weapon is drawn (see fig. 8, p. 30 above). The hilt is of gold, the high lights and shadows being painted over the gold leaf in white and mauve.

Two interesting points are noticeable: the large well-formed Brazil-nut pommel, and the long cross. It is too often taken for granted that at this date—about 990—no swords were furnished with long crosses like this, but only with the short thick guards found on most Viking or Carolingian swords. This hilt can be compared with those of the two INGELRIÍ swords previously mentioned.

In this same manuscript there are swords with Tea-Cosy pommels (fig. 48) and one with a two-part pommel of Petersen's Type N (one of the earlier Viking types of about 850 to 950) very accurately drawn in a scene of the beheading of John the Baptist (fig. 49). These three pictures seem also to be the work of the master of the Dedication page.

In a somewhat earlier manuscript, made in St. Gall during the first half of the 10th century,[6] we find a sword with a Brazil-nut pommel in a battle scene out of the Book of Kings. In the same picture appear two other X-type swords and one with a trilobate pommel.

Another Ottonian Dedication page is from a sacramentary made in Regensburg between 1002 and 1024 for Heinrich II.[7] Here we see again a sword with a large Brazil-nut pommel (fig. 49 below).

Another sword from the same manuscript is interesting because it shows how a large hand grasped the extremely short grips of these swords; the pommel, being quite flat, fits into the palm.

Throughout the 11th century both the Tea-Cosy and Brazil-nut pommels remained in use without any noticeable change in their shape, and while the various lobated

Fig. 49. From "The Gospels of Otto III".

[6] St. Gall MS, Cod. Perizoni 17, Leyden.
[7] Sacramentary of Heinrich II from Cathedral Treasury of Bamberg, Munich. Regensburg, 1002–1024, fol. 11.

types became less and less common a hitherto unknown type made its appearance for the first time. This was in the form of a disc.

It is not until we examine swords and monuments of the second half of the 12th century that we begin to see any noticeable change in the shape of the Brazil-nut pommel; at about that time it seems to have increased in depth or thickness at the base, so that it appears more conical when seen in profile. At the end of the century its height also began to increase until it became more like a peanut than a Brazil-nut (plate 4B).

There are some interesting examples of swords of different types shown in the work of some of the Rhenish artists who produced the many fine small altars of engraved copper-gilt during the first half of the 12th century. A figure of St. Simplicius (see fig. 10, p. 31 above) from one of these altars which was enamelled by an unknown craftsman of Hildesheim between 1100 and 1132[8] has a sword whose hilt is very similar to that of no. A.457 in the Wallace Collection.

Fig. 50. Swords from a copper-gilt altar. Hildesheim work, c. 1120.

Another, made by Rodkerus of Helmeshausen in 1118, gives us several portrayals of X-type pommels.[9] In the scenes which decorate the panels forming the sides and ends of this altar (the martyrdom of Paul and the baptism and death of Cornelius) several swords appear; all of their pommels are of the two X-types. In a group of three swords we can see (fig. 50) the three basic styles of the Brazil-nut form together—the semi-circular one with a straight upper edge, the wide shallow form with upper and lower edges curved equally, and the short stubby type. This group alone is evidence enough that the semi-circular style was not a late development but was contemporary with all the others, including the Tea-Cosy form. I think there is no doubt that the differences in the shapes of these pommels drawn by Rodkerus are deliberate, not accidental; his literal treatment of the weapons he portrays is shown by the inscriptions with which he has decorated some of their blades. These inscriptions are not in the form of names, as is the case with some other drawings of the same period, but of various apparently meaningless combinations of upright lines, crosses and circles, and in one case an interlaced pattern (figs. 51a and b).

[8] In the Victoria and Albert Museum.
[9] Falke, A. *Deutsche Schmelzarbeiten des Mittelalters*, Frankfurt, 1904, plates XII–XIV.

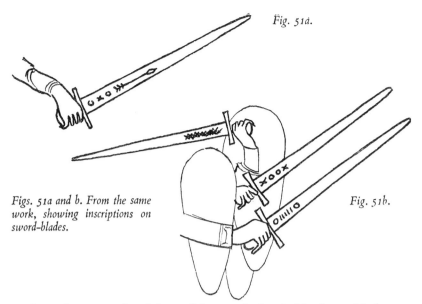

Fig. 51a.

Figs. 51a and b. From the same work, showing inscriptions on sword-blades.

Fig. 51b.

Countless swords of the Viking period exist[10] whose blades are inlaid with precisely the same odd assortment of symbols on one side and with smith-names on the other. The INGELRÍI sword in the British Museum is a case in point, for the reverse of its blade is inlaid with a cross potent between two groups of three upright strokes.[11] It is clear, then, that Rodkerus did not decorate his assassins' sword-blades with the first imaginary pattern which may have come into his head; he used marks which were probably still in common use in 1118, as they had been for two centuries before. By the same token we are entitled to assume that the pommels he drew were also taken from life.[12] Of the long narrow shape is a pommel from a figure of one of the Guards at the Sepulchre carved on a capital in the church at St. Nectaire; this is like the pommel on the left of the group on Rodkerus's altar, and is also very similar to the one carried by the elderly armour-bearer of the Dedication page of Otto III's Gospel Book.

From the beginning of the 12th century the regional division of the two main groups of the X-type pommels is no longer applicable. The Austrasian or Brazil-nut form seems entirely to have ousted the Tea-Cosy style in popular favour judging by the evidence of monuments, paintings, and actual swords which date

[10] R. Wegeli, "Inschriften auf mittelalterlichen Schwertklingen", Z.W.H.K., iii; and A. L. Lorange, *Den Yngre Jernalders Sverd*, Oslo, 1889.

[11] British Museum, no. 56.7–1.1404.

[12] For a note on this altar, see Z.W.H.K., viii. 8.

after about 1100. A possible reason for the preference shown for the Brazil-nut form and for its long survival is a very practical one. The straight lower edge and sharp rectangular corners of the Tea-Cosy pommel can be extremely uncomfortable when the weapon is in use, particularly if the user's hand is not too large for the grip, for the corner nearest to the wrist tends to jab into the angle made by the wrist and the edge of the hand when making a blow. In the Brazil-nut pommel this corner is curved away, following the curve made by the junction of the hand and wrist, into which it fits quite snugly. Thus it is not only more comfortable in use, but gives a firm support to the hand and acts as a fulcrum to help an upward swing of the sword. If the wielder's hand is too large for the grip, he can crook his little finger over the acutely pointed end of the pommel to secure a firm grasp of his weapon. These theories are based on practical tests made with swords having pommels of both Tea-Cosy and Brazil-nut forms, as well as on the evidence of contemporary art.

The second half of the 11th century brings us to the time where the Brazil-nut pommel begins to assume its final form, well exemplified by the "Sword of St. Maurice" in Vienna. Its particular interest lies in its great beauty of form, its restrained and simple decoration and its perfect condition; it seems to have been untouched by the hand of time (plate 5B).

The sword in the effigy of Count Dedo von Wettin in the Cathedral at Wechselburg is very similar[13] (fig. 52). Its proportions are almost identical except that its pommel is not quite so

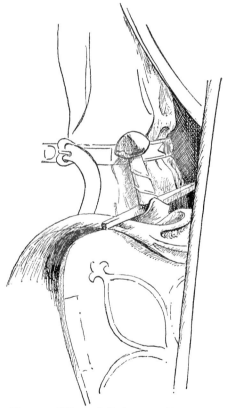

Fig. 52. Effigy of Dedo von Wettin, Wechselburg Cathedral, c. 1230.

[13] A. Goldschmidt, *Die Sculpturen von Freiburg und Wechselburg.*

Fig. 53. Sword from the Gudbransdal, Norway. Maidstone Museum.

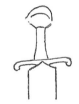

Fig. 54. From an Apocalypse, school of Matthew Paris, c. 1250.

tall. Another sword of approximately the same date is in the museum at Maidstone[14] (fig. 53), and a drawing from an Apocalypse of the school of Matthew Paris, of about 1250, shows an identical hilt[15] (fig. 54). Here we can set picture and original side by side to show their similarity.[16]

To illustrate the final phase of the Brazil-nut pommel there are no better examples than the swords portrayed in some of the finest sculptured figures of the 13th century, the statues of the Benefactors of Naumburg Cathedral in the West Choir.[17] These are justly regarded as some of the best pieces of German architectural sculpture of the Middle Ages. They rank with the figures on the west fronts of the cathedrals of Rheims and Paris, and in the south porch at Chartres, though they are not so well known. There is little doubt that the master craftsman who made them knew and was to some extent influenced by this French work of about 1240, though his own work is typical of all German medieval sculpture in that the figures are treated in a rather more literal and realistic manner than those of Paris or Chartres, though for our purpose this is one of their most useful qualities. In this group of statues there are seven swords.

Fig. 55. Count Hermann. Naumburg, c. 1250.

[14] Laking, Sir G., op. cit., I. 85, and fig. 106. A note has been found in the archives of the Maidstone Museum stating that this sword was found in the Gudbransdal in Norway, not near Maidstone as has previously been understood.

[15] An Apocalypse of the school of Matthew Paris, Bibliothèque Nationale, Paris, M.S.G. 403, fol. I.

[16] An impression of the first Great Seal of Richard I, on a document dated October 1189 in the Muniment Room at Westminster Abbey, has the sword-arm very well preserved, and shows a pommel of the more massively developed Brazil-nut form, similar to that of the Vienna sword.

[17] Kueas, H. *'Die Naumburger Werkstatt*, 1937.

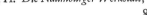

One has a disc and one a wheel pommel, and the remaining five have variant or developed forms of the late Brazil-nut types. It is possible to compare actual specimens of exactly the same kind—not merely similar weapons, but swords which might have been used by the sculptor as models for his work, so close is their resemblance to these sculptured swords.

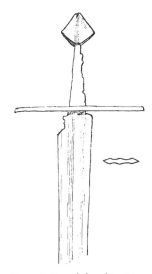

The sword of Count Hermann (fig. 55) has a pommel rather like that of the Vienna St. Maurice sword, only it has a strong vertical ridge down the middle. The pommel of Dietrich von Brehna's sword is the same, though not quite so wide (see fig. 16, p. 40 above). Both of

Fig. 56. Sword found in Hungary, cf. fig. 55.

these are distinguished from the St. Maurice sword's pommel by the straightness of the four sides and the sharpness of the angles. We can see that a sword (fig. 56) which was found in Hungary[18] is identical.

Before we deal with the last styles of Brazil-nut pommel we must return for a moment to the cocked-hat pommel which was mentioned earlier. In its original Scandinavian form it has been classified by Petersen under Type Y. It does not seem to have been quite so widely popular as the two X-types, though it was in use all through the 11th and 12th centuries and its development was parallel to that of the Brazil-nut type—that is, it became more massive towards the end of the 12th century and remained in use down to the end of the 13th (fig. 57). As a matter of fact we find representations of the final forms of this type at a later date than the last of the

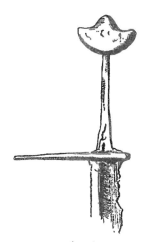

Fig. 57. Mid-13th century sword, Copenhagen.

[18] Szendrei, A. '*Ungarische Kriegsgeschichtliche Denkmaler*, Budapest, 1896.

Fig. 58. From a Goslar MS., c. 1230, cf. fig. 57.

X-type.[19] Figs. 58–60 show a few swords with this sort of pommel; from a Crucifixion scene in a manuscript from Goslar of about 1230[20] (fig. 58), and a sword, also found in Hungary (fig. 59) which has an identical pommel,[21] and another from Brunau (fig. 60) which is similar.[22]

Both these specimens have pommels broad at the base and rather tall and of a distinctly hat-like shape. The latest examples are to be seen in German manuscripts of the second half of the 13th century. A very late one (of about 1285) appears on the grave-slab of Ulrich von Regensburg at Zurich.[23]

Many of the large, developed Brazil-nut pommels of the mid-13th century seem to be a fusion of the two types: the Brazil-nut form—no longer very like a Brazil nut—tends to develop a slight concavity on its upper edges. The sword of Count Konrad at Naumburg is like this (fig. 61), and so is the pommel of an identical sword in the Royal Scottish Museum in Edinburgh whose finding-place is unfortunately not known (plate 12B).

Two more varieties of the Brazil-nut pommel are portrayed in the Naumburg figures. The sword of Wilhelm von Camburg has one shaped like a boat, though it is probably a variety of Brazil-nut type with the straight upper edge (fig. 62). One of the same shape may be seen on a sword in the Landesmuseum at Zurich.[24]

The figure of Count Dietmar shows a pommel which looks as if it has no connection with the Brazil-nut types; but I think it is none the less a logical development of the semi-circular type with a

Fig. 60. Sword found at Branau, mid-13th century.

Fig. 59. Sword found in Hungary, mid-13th century.

[19] B.M. MS. Add. 17687, c. 1280. Also shown in a manuscript of the Castle Library at Aschaffenburg (no. 13), c. 1250.

[20] "Der Goslar Evangeliar", fol. 10, Rathaus, Goslar, c. 1230.

[21] Szendrei, op. cit.

[22] Z.W.H.K., i. 3.

[23] Futterer, I. *Gotische Bildwerke der Deutschen Schweiz*, 1930.

[24] Landesmuseum, Zurich, No. A.G. 2765.

straight upper edge. It has become
more massive and much taller, almost
U-shaped, with a strong vertical mid-
rib (fig. 63).

These Naumburg sculptures can be
dated with some certainty. We know
that the West Choir of the cathedral,
of which they form a principal decoration, was nearing completion in 1249,
for in that year an appeal for funds to
enable the work to be completed was
sent out by the bishop; the fabric was
complete, and it was the decoration
which was held up. This must have
included these statues of the bene-

Fig. 61. Count Conrad, Naumburg,
c. 1250.

factors, so it seems probable that they were made between 1249
and about 1255.[25]

The seven swords in the hands of these figures show very
clearly some of the pommels in use during the 13th century, and
probably represent the latest dated examples of the Brazil-nut
forms.

Another very rich source of pictured examples of this pommel-
form is that very fine book of Old Testament stories made about
1250 and illustrated by an artist of exceptional ability, probably
a Frenchman,[26] the Maciejowski Bible. These illustrations are
possibly without exception the finest book-paintings from a
military point of view so far known to us. It has often been suggested, and it does seem very likely, that the artist himself had
been a soldier, so meticulously accurate are all his drawings of
every item of military gear from siege-engines to cross-bow bolts
and tent-pegs. Also, his battle scenes tend generally to be better
than his more peaceful ones, and give the impression that he has
really let himself go on a subject he knows and enjoys.

The very excellence of these pictures has in a way hindered the
proper study of the Brazil-nut pommel, for they have so often
been brought forward by writers on medieval arms as proof that

[25] Kueas, H. op. cit.
[26] Cockerell, Sir S. *A Picture Book of Old Testament Stories of the Thirteenth Century*
(Roxburghe Club), 1927.

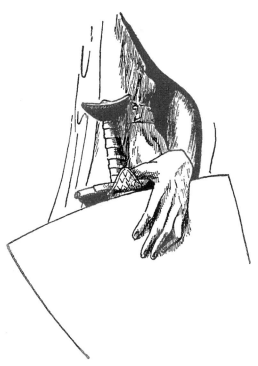

Fig. 62. Wilhelm von Camburg, Naumburg, c. 1250.

this pommel was essentially a 13th-century type; its very perfection seems to have blinded them to the mass of evidence contained in earlier works which shows beyond doubt that this form originated in the 10th century and was the pommel *par excellence* of the 11th; those shown in these Old Testament pictures in fact portray only the last stages in the development of a type which had its origin three full centuries earlier.

These Brazil-nut pommels and their later developed forms may be separated into six types, A to F. The prototype, first found in definite Viking contexts, should still be called Type X since Petersen has thus immortalised it. First datable by grave finds[27] at *c.* 950, there are manuscript drawings of an even earlier date which show it,[28] and later documents show that it still seems to have been in use *c.* 1125.[29]

[27] See note 8, chap. 1.
[28] Codex perizoni 17, op. cit.
[29] e.g. a sculptured capital at St. Nectaire. (Note 14, chap. 1.)

Type A. A development of X, with the ends extended to form a very wide pommel, often as much as about 4" across. The earliest datable examples, clearly shown, are from an Arpad grave-find in Hungary of *c.* 1000, and a drawing (see fig. 8, p. 30 above) in an Ottonian manuscript picture datable between 983–99.[30] It probably remained popular until *c.* 1150 (plates 2A and 4C).

A

Type B. This is bulkier and shorter and rounder than A, being a stouter version of X. Never very common, it seems mostly to be found on swords which on other evidence, i.e. blade inscriptions, can be dated between *c.* 1050 and *c.* 1150 (plate 4B).

B

Type C. The pommel found on Viking swords of Type IX, like a cocked hat (Petersen's Type Y)[31] is the immediate ancestor of C, which is of a similar hat-shape, but taller in the "crown" and now made in one piece (fig. 59). It is shown in art up to about 1150, merging after that time with:

C

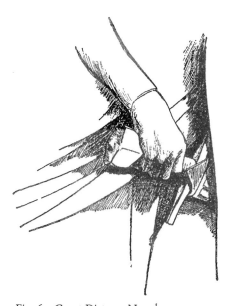

Fig. 63. Count Dietmar, Naumburg, c. 1250.

[30] Cod. lat. 4453, op. cit.
[31] See note 8, chap. 1.

Type D. A stouter, bulkier version of C. Most frequently found in painting and sculpture between *c.* 1225 and *c.* 1275, and upon surviving swords which seem to be of the same date (see fig. 60, p. 90 above).

Type E. Similar to D in bulk, it has straight or only slightly dished upper edges. Sometimes has a pronounced mid-rib (fig. 61). Contemporary with D (see plate 12B).

Type F. A more angular form of E, which seems to have been popular throughout the period 1175–1275. (plate 8C). Sometimes has a pronounced mid-rib.

The other pommel form which Petersen classified also under Type X is the "Mushroom" or "Tea-Cosy" pommel. It seems to have had far less popularity after the end of the Viking Age than the Brazil-nut form. Some of its earlier forms were definitely "Pilzformige" like certain kinds of toadstools, and this fungoid shape is still found—very massive—in the 11th century. This should be classified as:

Type B1. It bears some resemblance to the B pommels but with a straight lower edge. Good examples are in the Tower of London and the Historisches Museum in Berne (fig. 1).[32]

[32] Historisches Museum, Berne. Inv. no. 840·5.

Fig. 1

The disc-form of pommel, first used during the 10th century, was as predominant between *c.* 1150–*c.* 1400 as the Brazil-nut had been earlier. It has long been believed that the plain disc came first, and that all pommels of the so-called "wheel" form were later developments of it, and thus later in sequence. This may not be entirely so. Among many swords recently found in Finland[33] in graves of the latest Viking period (*c.* 980–1000) there were pommels of the wheel-forms H and I as well as of the plain disc-form G. Further evidence for the use of the disc or wheel-form during the 10th century comes from an Ottonian manuscript of Otto III,[34] where a figure of a member of Herod's bodyguard is shown with one. Its latest use was well on into the 16th century.

The disc and wheel pommels fall into five types and three later sub-types.

Type G. A plain disc, usually slightly convex on its two faces and varying between $\frac{1}{2}''$ and $1''$ thick. Some examples, mostly dating after 1400, have concave faces. This pommel type is often found on swords of Types X and XI (plates 2B and 5A).

G

Type H. Here the edges of the disc are chamfered off on each face, giving a low prominence on either side, the inner, flat faces being about $\frac{1}{4}$ less in diameter than the outer rim. Perhaps the commonest of all medieval pommels, it is found on swords of every type from the 10th century until the early 15th, and after three-quarters of a century of apparent unpopularity it again appears, rarely, between *c.* 1500–1525.

H

[33] Information given me in the course of correspondence with Dr. Jorma Leppaho of Helsinki, who found them.
[34] Gotha, Landsbibliothek. Cod. 1.19.

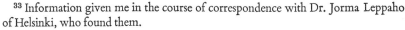

Type I.   The inner disc is much smaller than in H, the chamfered edges are wider and the whole pommel is much deeper from front to back. The type was found among those Viking swords in Finland previously mentioned, but its real popularity seems to have begun in about the middle years of the 13th century. In many examples the faces are hollowed out to hold little plates, most of which are now missing, of gold or silver or enamel (plate 13).

Type J.   Similar to I, but the sloping faces are deeply hollowed out. This type is seldom found in swords earlier in date than *c.* 1250, or in ones later than *c.* 1425 (e.g. plates 11B and 23).

Type K.   A very wide and flat variety of J. Rare before *c.* 1260, fairly common (particularly in art) between *c.* 1290–1350, and rare after that until *c.* 1480 (plates 19B and 28A; fig. 28). Often of oval shape (plates 29 and 47).

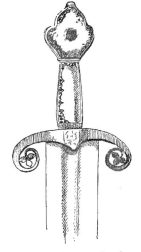

Fig. 64. The sword of St. Ferdinand, Madrid.

Such are the two main groupings of pommels applying mainly to the swords in Group I. Though nine swords out of ten dating between *c.* 950 and 1350 are fitted with one or other of these types, there are a number of other forms which by the infrequency of their appearance in art or in fact cannot be placed in the main classifications. These are as follows:

96

Type L.   A sort of tall, angular trefoil. The only example I know
            of is a splendid sword in the Armeria Real in Madrid,
            said to have belonged to Ferdinand III (St. Ferdinand)
            of Castile, reg. 1223–1253 (fig. 64). Similar pommels
            are to be seen in Spanish manuscript pictures of the
            12th and 13th centuries, e.g. a manuscript of St. Beato
            de Liebana's commentaries on the Apocalypse in the
            British Museum (1109). From the rarity of its appear-
            ance elsewhere it may perhaps be said to be a type of
            Spanish fashion.

L

Type M.   On the other hand this might be said to be as dis-
            tinctively British. A late developed survival of the
            multi-lobed Viking pommel-form, it is found with
            some frequency on monuments in northern England
            and southern Scotland dating between *c.* 1250 and
            1350. Examples are the De Sulney monument at
            Newton Solney in Derbyshire,[35] the effigy of a de
            L'Isle at Rampton in Cambridgeshire,[36] the wooden
            effigy of Robert of Normandy in Gloucester Cathe-
            dral,[37] a knight in Cartmel Priory, Lancs.,[38] and many
            others, as well as a number of unrecorded grave slabs
            in Westmorland and the better known one at Ebber-
            ston in the North Riding of Yorkshire.[39] Several
            others, rather later in date, from Scotland have been
            thoroughly recorded.

M

                There are a few surviving examples. One, in the
            museum in Oslo (plate 3D) found in a grave at
            Korsoygaden near that city has the rare distinction of a
            clearly-readable runic inscription on one of the fillets
            of bronze which bound the now missing grip. It is
            remarkably similar to a fine sword found in the River
            Ouse near Cawood in Yorkshire, now in an English
            private collection (plate 3C). In the same collection is

---

[35] Hewitt, op. cit., vol. I, p. 261, pl. LXIV.
[36] Stothard, op. cit.
[37] ibid.
[38] Antiquaries' Journal, 1943, vol. XXIII, nos. 1, 2.
[39] Bruhn Hoffmeyer, op. cit., plate IIIb; also Antiquaries' Journal, 1938, vol. XVIII.

Fig. 65. St. George, west front, Freiburg Cathedral, c. 1300.

a boy's sword of *c.* 1300, with a similar pommel made in a simpler fashion.[40] The Korsoygaden sword, long believed to be of late Viking date, is in fact a Type XII. The hilt is almost exactly the same shape as that of the Cawood sword (also a XII), which by the style of the inlaid inscriptions in its blade may be placed with some confidence within a period between perhaps 1240 and 1310.[41] Certainly no earlier than the former. The runes on the Korsoygaden hilt might have been made at any time between 1000 and 1300 (not later). Thus, in spite of its being found in a stone coffin with the remains of a circular shield, it seems likely that the Korsoygaden sword must be of *c.* 1240–1300, not of *c.* 1000. Circular shields continued in very popular use in Scandinavia right through the Middle Ages, many well-preserved ones still surviving.[42]

Similarly, a so-called Viking sword in the British Museum ought to be dated within the 13th century instead of the Viking Age. Here the pommel is of similar character to the Cawood and Korsoygaden swords, but the cross is of a far more Viking-like shape, like many upon swords of Petersen's Type Z. The blade (part of which is missing) could be of Type X, but it seems more like a XII. However, it has an inscription inlaid in tiny white-metal letters which is of a distinctively later character than any Viking inscription.[43]

Type N. A pommel shaped like a boat. Examples are rare; there is one in the Zweizerische Landesmuseum in Zurich (Type XIIIa) and a second is in private hands in Rumania. This also is of Type XIIIa, a very large one. In art it is not quite so rare—for instance, one of the Benefactors of Naumburg has one (Wilhelm von Camburg) on a short sword of Type XIV (see fig. 62, p. 92 above).

N

---

[40] Both in the collection of Mrs. How; the boy's sword was formerly in my own.
[41] Wegeli, op. cit.
[42] Many are described and illustrated in "Nordisk Kultur: Vapen", XIIb, Stockholm.
[43] Wegeli, op. cit.

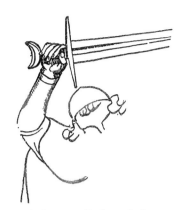

Fig. 66. St. Peter, Freiburg Cathedral.

Fig. 67. One of the sleeping guards from the Easter Sepulchre, Freiburg.

Type O. Another rare type, but, curiously, nearly every sculptured figure of a military kind in the Cathedral of Freiburg has one of them—St. George and St. Sebastian, the sleeping guards at the Sepulchre, St. Peter in the Garden of Gethsemane and many more (figs. 65, 66, 67). Actual examples are almost unknown. There is a photograph of one in the catalogue of the Gimbel Collection. Even the never-failing Maciejowski Bible only shows one of them.

Type P. There seems to be only a solitary example of this, on the sword of another of the Naumburg Benefactors, Dietmar von Kisteritz (see fig. 63, p. 93 above).

Type Q. There are several examples in manuscript paintings dating between c. 1280–c. 1325, but no known survivors. In the manuscripts they generally appear on swords of Type XIV (fig. 68).

Fig. 68. Sword of Type XIV, with Type Q pommel. From an E. Anglian MS., c. 1310, Emmanuel College, Cambridge.

R

Type R. A spherical pommel, survivors being more rare than one might expect of such an obviously practical form of pommel. Two are in the London Museum, the first on a sword of Viking type where it looks most incongruous, yet it is no replacement. It has a simple decoration of floral sprigs in the manner of many 9th–10th century swords of Frankish origin. The second spherical pommel is on a fine sword of Type XVI of *c.* 1300 which was found in Cannon Street in London. In the Maciejowski Bible the drawing of Goliath shows a pommel of exactly similar form and decoration (fig. 69).

S

Type S. This type, a cube with the corners bevelled off, is less rare than the preceding types as far as survivors go, but is less frequently shown in art. There seems to be only one sculptured example, on an effigy in the church at Halton Holgate in Lincolnshire, dating about 1320. Here the sculptured sword is a Type XIIIa (fig. 70). Of the same type are most of the actual survivors. There are three in Stockholm, two XIIIa's and one XIIIb, while a similar but much finer XIIIa used to be in the Boissonas Collection at Geneva, though its present whereabouts is unknown to me (fig. 71).

There is another pommel which must be noted with the preceding nineteen types, but as it has only been observed to be a distinct type since the original form of this typology was published in 1960, it cannot follow as it should in the sequence, and become Type T; it must take its place at the end of the line, as it were, and be classified as Type W. Because its only appearances so far observed are on swords dating before 1350, it must go into the typology at this point.

W

Type W. This is of a form difficult to describe; it may be likened to a squashed-up variety of one of the discoid pommels, or it might be likened to certain forms of seed-pods—though to call it "pod-shaped" could be misleading, as it is quite unlike a pea or a bean pod, the things one immediately visualizes as being pod-shaped.

Until 1961 the only examples noted were on the Type XVI sword at Lincoln (plate 26A) and on a boy's sword in the Glasgow Museum. But since then three others have come to my notice, and a close inspection of an effigy at Gosberton in Lincolnshire positively confirmed a good, unmistakable representation of one in art. Stothard's drawing of this effigy, and a photograph reproduced by Prior and Gardner, show what appears to be a vaguely spherical pommel; but the stone itself shows a very well-cut (and well-preserved) pommel of Type W. There is another from the V. Gay Collection in the Museum für Deutsche Geschichte, Berlin.

A dagger in the collection of the late Sir James Mann has one of these, but it had never been published or compared with the Lincoln one. Then in 1961 and 1962 two remarkable examples appeared in the sale-room. One is

Fig. 69. Goliath, from the Maciejowski Bible.

on a tiny, charming little sword made for a boy of about seven years old,[44] the other on a most beautiful example of Type XIV (plate 20A).[45] The blade bears rather an unusual inscription—the letters TOTO (or IOIO) framed in half-circles, repeated in opposition twice on either face of the blade. Whether the consonants are I's or T's is impossible to determine. While the word "Toto" used as a motto (as on a ring) is entirely consistent with 14th century custom, so too would be the initials I and O if they were used as an invocation: O IESUS—though in this case one would expect the O's to precede the I's. It seems that "Toto" is a more likely reading.

These 20 pommel forms are all to be found, in art and in reality, on swords of Group I dating between 1100–1350, though as we

---

[44] In the collection of Mrs. How.

[45] Until 1929 in the De Cosson Collection (catalogue: Sotheby's, May 14th, 1929, lot 93; and Sotheby's, Nov. 30th, 1962, lot 30, collection of John Wallace Esq.).

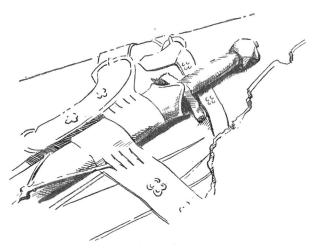

Fig. 70. Effigy at Halton Holgate, Lincs., c. 1310.

have seen many went right through to the 16th century with the Group II swords. But there are further pommel types which did not come into use at all until after *c.* 1350 and which are exclusively associated with swords of Group II. The first of these late pommels are all bye-forms of the disc pommels.

Type G1. This does not appear until the second quarter of the 15th century, and seems (on the evidence so far available) to be of a purely Italian style. The faces of the disc are strongly convex, so that it often gives the appearance of a slightly flattened globe rather than a blown-out disc. Each face bears an elaborate flower-like design milled out of the surface in a series of intersecting arcs. A very good example of this pommel is shown in plate 46D and Frontispiece.

Type G2. In basic form similar to G1, and contemporary with it, this has decoration in the form of radiating flutings in the form of a cockle-shell (plate 44C). This too is distinctly Italian in its usage.

Type H1. First appears *c.* 1350, and seems to have gone out of favour by the first quarter of the 15th century. It is always very flat, and is oval in form, never circular. The edges are chamfered off, very shallowly (plate 30B). Sometimes these profiles are flat, more often strongly concave. There are innumerable examples of

102

the type; one is shown at plate 30B, and a sculptured specimen from the tomb-effigy of Gunther von Schwarzburg (+1349) in fig. 72.

Type I1. Simply the profiled disc or "wheel" form cut into a hexagonal or octagonal shape by faceting the profile. Actually this one was used upon swords of Group I, though the period of its greatest popularity was *c.* 1360–*c.* 1440–50. The earliest datable example is the sword found in the tomb of the Emperor Albrecht I *ob.* 1308 (see fig. 34, p. 63). A good example in sculpture is the monumental figure of Bishop Gerhard Von Schwarzburg (1400) in Wurzburg Cathedral (fig. 73). Very many appear on English brasses between *c.* 1360–1435 (fig. 74). Most surviving examples are of bronze or latten.

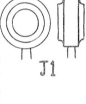

Type J1. This is an elaborated form of the classic wheel pommel. Its best exemplar is a sword of Type XVIII preserved in the library of the Abbey of Westminster, a most beautiful weapon which is associated with the name of King Henry V (fig. 75). This is no mere funerary object, but a magnificent fighting sword (bearing upon its still sharp edges much indication of use) which comes to life in one's hand. The pommel is very massive, but its weight is kept down because only the central thick disc is of solid iron; the raised rims are beaten out of thin iron and brazed on to the main part of the pommel. A similar pommel is in the University Museum of Ethnology and Archaeology at Cambridge on a good sword (Type XV) of about the same period as the Westminster one, but here the pommel is smaller, and of solid bronze (plate 25). Many of these pommels are shown on English brasses dating between *c.* 1420–*c.* 1450, so much so that it is tempting to suppose that this may be a distinctively English type (fig. 76).

Fig. 71. Sword of Type XIIIa, ex. Boissonas Collection.

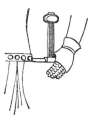

Fig. 72. Effigy of
Gunther von
Schwarzburg,
Frankfurt, 1349.

From the variants of the old disc-forms we come to the completely new shapes of the 15th century. All of these seem to derive from a single basic form which has been variously described as of "fig", "pear" or "scent-stopper" form. The last is much more descriptive of the shape. There are five direct variants of this scent-stopper pommel, and two others which are closely akin. Though the first variety of the scent-stopper appears early in the 14th century (plate 20B), its real usage did not start until *c.* 1360, while its variants continued in use far into the 16th century. Carrying straight on from the Group I typology, the scent-stopper form becomes:

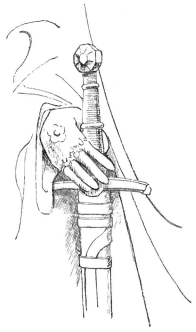

Fig. 73. Effigy of Bishop Gerhard von Schwarzburg, Wurzburg Cathedral, 1400.

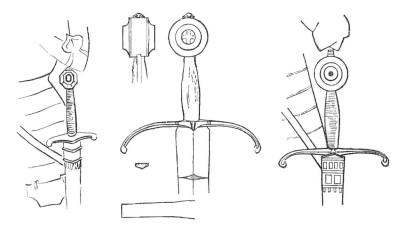

Fig. 74. Brass of Sir John de Leventhorpe, 1433, Saw-bridgeworth, Herts.

Fig. 75. Sword of Henry V, Westminster Abbey.

Fig. 76. Brass of Richard Fox, Arkesden, Essex, 1430.

Type T. This is generally faceted in vertical panels, hence the name, though there are plenty of plain examples circular in plan.

T

Type T1. In the form of a truncated wedge. Though it may in fact have been the prototype of all later T-class pommels, it is so rare that it seems more suitable to classify it as a bye-form of T.

T1

Type T2. A very handsome pommel which, on the evidence of monuments, seems to have been popular in England and Germany during the years between 1360–1420. The classic and well-known example is that magnificent sword now in the Fitzwilliam Museum at Cambridge, found in the River Cam. A similar sword of slightly smaller and more manageable proportions— the Cambridge sword is particularly big—is in the collection of Mr. R. T. Gwynn of Epsom. One of the best monumental ones is on the effigy in Arnstadt of Gunther von Schwarzburg (1368) (fig. 77). The swords found in the Abbey Church of Konigsfeld in the graves of those two knights, Friedrich von Griffenstein and Frederiks von Tarant, who fell in the battle of Sempach (1386) have pommels of this type,

T2

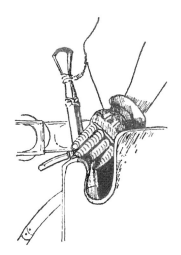

Fig. 77. Effigy of a later Gunther von Schwarzburg, Arnstadt, 1368.

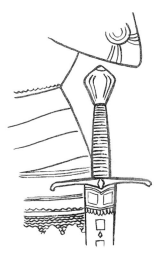

Fig. 78. Brass of Sir Thomas Braunstone Wisbech, Cambridge, 1401.

and like all other swords upon which it is found are of Type XVII.

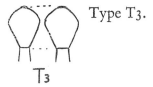

Type T3. A squatter variety which could well be described as fig-shaped. It is often plain, but many shown on English brasses *c.* 1400 – 1440 are closely ribbed (fig. 78 and plate 43B). It seems rarely to be found after about 1430, and seldom before 1400; and though most monumental examples of it are English, most surviving swords fitted with it have characteristically Italian features. This, however, is not surprising, since most English armour and weapons of this period seem to owe a great deal to the styles of the Italian armourers and weaponsmiths. These pommels, when found, seem mostly to be fitted to swords of Type XVIII.

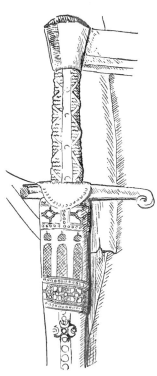

Fig. 79. Effigy of Sir John Wyard, Meriden, Warwick, 1411.

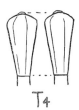

Type T4. Simply a much elongated form of T, in which the upper cone is very flattened so that the pommel rather resembles a cork, as in the effigy of Sir John Wyard (1411) in the Church of Meriden in Warwickshire (fig. 79), and the figure of Pierre de Navarre, Count of Evreux, in the stained-glass window in Evreux Cathedral (*c.* 1390, fig. 80).

Type T5. A pear-shaped variant, and of later usage than most of the others. This is the one which is most often found upon swords which one would hesitate to date earlier than 1500, i.e. two in the Wallace Collection in London (nos. A504 and A698), though it is seen on English monuments (as in the brass of Sir John Peyrent) as early as the 1420's (figs. 81, 82).

Type U. This can perhaps vaguely be called "key-shaped" as it resembles nothing so much as those 19th-century watch-keys. Some of the handsomest pommels ever made, painted or sculpted are of this form, which dates throughout the whole of the last three-quarters of the 15th century. There are notable examples: a beautiful sword in the Zweizerisches Landesmuseum in Zurich (fig. 83), which though it has a typical hilt of the 1450's is furnished with a flat, broad, fullered blade of the kind we would expect to find on a sword of Type XII; a painting by a Flemish master of *c.* 1470 in the collection of Her Majesty the Queen shows another (fig. 84), and there are several on German tomb effigies of the late 15th century, notably that of Bishop Johannes von Grumbach, *c.* 1475 (fig. 85).

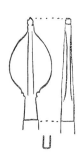

Fig. 80. Sword of Pierre de Navarre, Count of Evreux, from a window in Evreux Cathedral, c. 1390.

Fig. 81. Brass of Sir John Peyrent, Digswell, Herts., 1415.

Fig. 82. Brass of W. Swetenham, Blakesey, Northants, c. 1430.

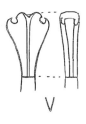

Type V is of a very distinctive form, usually and not altogether misleadingly described as "fish-tail". There are few examples, all on particularly fine swords. The best is in the Wallace Collection in London (plate 36A). Another is in the Musée de Cluny (fig. 88), while a third is in my own collection (plate 36B). These swords are homogeneous single-handed weapons, but there is a V1 pommel on a two-hand sword of Charles V in the Armeria Real at Madrid; this is an old, but not original, association. A fifth is a sword in excavated condition in Zurich (fig. 87). These, so far,

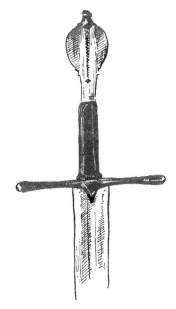

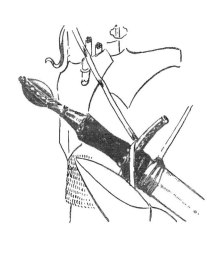

Fig. 83. Sword in the Landesmuseum, Zurich.

Fig. 84. From "The Trinity College Altarpiece". Flemish, c. 1475. Collection of H.M. The Queen. National Gallery of Scotland.

Fig. 85. Effigy of Bishop Johannes von Grumbach, c. 1475.

seem to be the only survivors. The type is less rare in art. There is a German effigy at Dongsdorff in Wurttemberg of Ulrich von Hohenrechburg (+1458) which shows one (fig. 86), and in England we have three most splendid examples in the alabaster effigies of William Phillipp, Lord Berdolph (+1441) in Dennington Church, Suffolk;[46] of an unidentified knight at Porlock, Somerset (c. 1440), and of Reginald, third Lord Cobham (+1446) at Lingfield in Surrey.[47] A drawing in one of the versions of "The Warwick Roll" of c. 1483 shows the Kingmaker holding a sword very similar to that shown on plate 36B, while in the National Gallery in London is a painting of "The Virgin and St. George" by Hans Memling with a similar pommel. Several other Flemish and German paintings show this pommel type, so much so that it is not unreasonable to suggest that it is a North-Western European rather than an Italian type.

[46] Stothard, op. cit.
[47] Gardner, A., Alabaster Tombs, 1940, no. 205.

Type V1. Here the concave, flowing edges of the sides of the pommel flare out more strongly, and the top is not cut into the curves peculiar to Type V. This is as distinctively Italian, at least on the evidence of art, as Type V is not. Many paintings by Gentile de Fabriano show the type, mostly dating between *c.* 1420–35; notably his Adoration of the Magi in the Uffizi Gallery in Florence, and his St. George in the same gallery, one of four figures of saints on an altarpiece. Actual examples are rare. A particularly fine one, though not on a fighting sword, is on the silver-gilt hilt of the "Pearl" sword of the City of Bristol, a ceremonial weapon presented to that city in 1431 by Sir John de Wells. A more down-to-earth but no less magnificent one is a sword now in the possession of Mr. C. O. von Kienbusch in New York. It is of Type XV and dates late in the 15th century. Formerly in the Bernal and Morgan Williams collections, it is so well-known that it needs no introduction here.

V1

Type V2 is as it were a rounded and blunted version of V1. Four examples survive: the corporation sword given by Edward IV to the City of Coventry; taken away again by him in 1471 after Coventry had sided with the Lancastrian rebels, lost for four centuries until its hilt turned up in a rubbish heap whence it got into the collection of Sir Guy Laking, sold in 1921 and now in the Burrell Collection, Glasgow.[48] Other civic swords, notably the "Steel" sword of the City of Hereford, have similar pommels. The most useful example in sculpture is on the Beaufort tomb in Canterbury Cathedral, where the Lady Margaret Holland (+1439) lies between her first and second husbands; John Beaufort, Earl of Somerset (+1410) and Thomas, Duke of Clarence and brother of Henry V, killed in the disaster of Beaugé in 1421. Both figures are identical, and each sword has a V2 pommel. Another is shown in the hand of a St. Catherine in a painting of a Calvary by a Flemish master in the Cathedral of St. Sauveur at

V2

[48] Laking, op. cit., vol. II, p. 319, fig. 698.

Bruges (fig. 89). The hilt of this sword, though the painting dates *c.* 1400, is remarkably similar to the Coventry hilt.

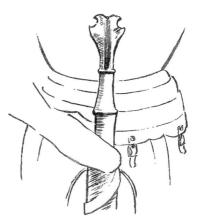

Fig. 86. Effigy of Ulrich von Hohenrech-burg. Dongsdorff, Wurttemberg, +1458.

Z

Type Z. Unlike Type W, there are hundreds of examples of this. Its first use (as far as we can tell at present) seems to have been *c.* 1300, on a "Great Sword" of Type

Fig. 87. Sword in the Landesmuseum, Zurich. Type XVIIIa.

Fig. 88. Sword in the Musée de Cluny.

XIIIa,[49] but mostly it seems to have been popular after *c.* 1430. Great numbers of them may be seen on

[49] Z.H.W.K., 1, 4.

swords still preserved in the Arsenal at Venice. There was an outstanding example of one of these in the 1929 sale of the de Cosson Collection, lot 97: "A very fine Venetian sword. This is one of the many swords of the same type made for the Council of Ten and preserved in the Ducal Palace at Venice; some have C.X. stamped on their leather grips."[50] Others (such as a fine one in the Kienbusch Collection, plate 41), have been found in old Venetian territory, or in Hungary. In spite of the number found north of the Danube, it does seem to be of distinctively Venetian type. This supposition is strengthened by the type's survival into the 18th century as the most common form of pommel upon the Venetian broadsword called "Schiavona", a form of sword used by the Venetian Stradiots recruited from Dalmatia.

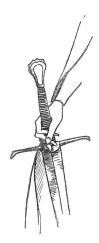

Fig. 89. From a Flemish painting in the Cathedral of St. Sauveur, Bruges, c. 1400.

[50] De Cosson, Sotheby's, May 14th, 1929, lot 97, pl. 1. The descriptions in this Catalogue were written by De Cosson himself before his death.

CHAPTER FOUR

Cross-Guards

THE cross-guard of a medieval sword is more often known, incorrectly, as the "Quillons". As far as we know at present, the earliest use of this term is not medieval, but as late as *c.* 1570,[1] so in accordance with the modern practice of referring to pieces of armour and arms by their contemporary English names, this feature of the sword should be called simply "the cross".

Fig. 90.
9th century sword
from Askeaton,
Co. Limerick.

In the past hundred years or so it has been assumed (and too often written) that the cross of a medieval sword provides clear and reliable indication of date.[2] Recent research has shown, however, that this is not so; a sword's cross, taken on its own, tells us nothing. For instance, a style which has always been taken confidently to be exclusive to the period 1380–1450 is found on an 8th–9th century Viking sword in a grave at Askeaton, Co. Limerick,[3] (fig. 90); another, too often held to belong only to the late 15th–early 16th centuries, is to be seen perfectly clearly in manuscript pictures of the 12th and 13th centuries[4] (fig. 91), and in English brasses of the early 15th century[5] (figs. 74, 76).

Other styles which have been assumed to indicate a 12th or 13th

---

[1] Statute des Fourbisseurs de Nantes, 1570 (Gay, Victor, *Glossaire Archaeologique*, vol. II, p. 281).

[2] e.g. London Museum Mediaeval Catalogue, 1940, p. 28. "The Quillons are in fact an important dating criterion . . ." See also Bruhn Hoffmeyer, *Middelalderens Tvaeeggede Sverd* (English Summary), Copenhagen, 1954, vol. 1, p. 181.

[3] Davidson, Dr. H. R. E., *The Sword in Anglo-Saxon England*, pl. 54–55 and fig. 82.

[4] e.g. The Winchester Bible, *c.* 1170; a psalter, *c.* 1250, in the library of the Duke of Rutland.

[5] e.g. Richard Fox, Arkesdon, Essex, 1430; Sir John de Harpeden, Westminster Abbey, 1433; Sir John de Leventhorpe, Sawbridgeworth, Herts., 1433; Sir John Wingfield, Letheringham, Suffolk, 1401; Sir Robert Swinborne, Little Horkesley, Essex, 1391, etc.

century date appear on swords of the 15th and 16th. But in spite of its invalidity as a dating criterion, the cross can be classified into 11 basic styles. Such a classification is of some value, even though the majority of the styles span the entire medieval period.

Most crosses are quite plain, but upon a few personal taste has been exercised to vary detail; the extremities may be decorated with indentations, swellings and variously shaped knobs; the écussons (that part of the cross between the arms, into which the blade is set on the underside and upon which the grip fits on the upper) may be decorated with incised lines, flutings, engraving and so on, while the arms may be fluted, gadrooned, twisted, or even in a few cases tortured into strange twig-like forms reminiscent of (indeed, identical with) the "crabstock" handles and spouts of English 18th-century Staffordshire earthenware teapots. In spite of the endless possibilities of decoration, there are only the 11 basic forms.

Fig. 91. From a mid-13th century psalter, Library of the Duke of Rutland.

After about 1350 we may expect to find certain fashionable trends, and in rare cases national or regional characteristics.[6]

The first series, Styles 1 to 7, are to be found mostly on swords of Group I; the second series of Styles 8 to 11 are found—or have so far been found—only on surviving swords of Group II.

Style 1. A simple and obvious form, a straight bar tapering slightly toward the ends. First found in Viking graves of the 10th century[7] the Vikings had a name for it: "Gaddhjalt" (Spike-Hilt).[8] It was still in use in the Renaissance (plates 1C, 6A and 46B). Generally square in section, it may sometimes be circular, or in rare, late cases octagonal.

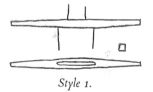

Style 1.

Style 1a. A less sophisticated version of 1, being just a plain straight rod expanding in the écusson to accommodate the tang. In section it can be square (plate 29) or circular (plate 31) or octagonal (plate 28B). It was in continuous use from the 11th century until the 17th.

[6] See Bruhn Hoffmeyer, op. cit., plates XXXV, XXXVI, XXXVIII.
[7] Petersen, op. cit.
[8] Shetelig, H., Scandinavian Archaeology, 1937.

113

Style 2.

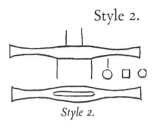

Style 2.

More elaborate. The central portion is strong and solidly rectangular; the arms are waisted and expand at the ends. The section is most often square, but when it is, the edges are rounded off, but the écusson is nearly always sharply squared off. Sometimes the section of the arms is circular, sometimes octagonal, but in these cases the écusson remains rectangular. In rare cases the écusson may be decorated with a small appendage protruding over the blade (fig. 92).

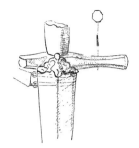

Fig. 92. Effigy of Sir John Savage, 1463. Macclesfield, Cheshire.

Style 3.

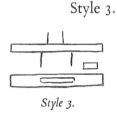

Style 3.

As simple as 1, a solid, stout bar always of flat rectangular section, always rather short. The edges are sharply squared, except where they have been marred by corrosion. It was very popular during the periods *c.* 1150–1250 and *c.* 1380–1430 (figs. 81 and 82).

These three styles are rarely decorated, even in late examples.

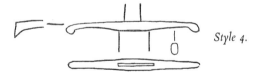

Style 4.

Style 4.

Similar to 1 but with downturned tips. These ends may be cut off square at the top and the end and curved away into the arm on the underside (fig. 94) or knobbed (plate 3B).

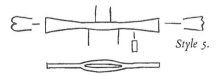

Style 5.

Style 5.

Somewhat resembles a bow-tie. The arms are very flat in plan and broad in elevation, widening at the ends. There are perhaps more decorative variations to this style than to any other. The tips are often embellished with one or more indentations (plate 13) or perforations (plate 26C). In late examples the section may be a flattened hexagon (plate 36B) and the écusson, in these late ones, is usually drawn down over the blade in a sharp cusped point (plate 38).

Though most surviving examples of the first form of these styles are straight, they may equally well be curved, and often are, for with such simple forms, little more than short rods of iron, curvature could easily be applied by the sword-cutler if the personal taste of his customer called for it. There are many examples of curved crosses of Style 1 and 1a (plates 14C and 46B) and a few rare ones of Style 2; one very unusual example in the Armouries of the Tower of London has one arm curved slightly upwards and the other correspondingly down, a reverse curve which is normally only associated with 16th century sword-hilts.

Fig. 93. Brass of Sir Robert de Septvans, Chart, Kent, 1306.

Style 3, being so short and solid, is rarely curved, while Style 5, by the very nature of its construction, can never be curved. There are however two further styles of these Group I crosses which are clearly always made curved:

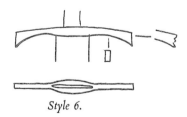

Style 6.

Style 6. A curved version of 5. For obvious reasons 5 cannot be curved after being made; any curved variety must be forged that way to begin with, hence Style 6. Decorative treatment is the same as may be applied to 5. A noticeable feature about the form of crosses of these styles 5 and 6 is that the underside, nearest the

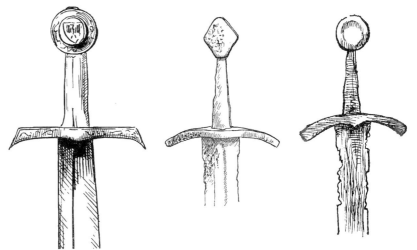

Fig. 94. "The Conyers Falchion", Durham Cathedral, c. 1250.

Fig. 95. Sword, c. 1200, ex. Dreger Collection.

Fig. 96. Sword, c. 1250, Museum of Archaeology, Cambridge (cf. fig. 97).

blade, is more strongly arched on each arm than the upper side (figs. 95–97 and plates 5A, 7, 18, 26A and B).

Style 7.

Style 7.   In elevation this looks like a curved 1, but it is quite different. In plan it is broad, giving a ribbon-like section with the broad face set at right angles to the plane of the blade. The ends are generally plain (plate 2B and figs. 81 and 93).

In some examples of Styles 6 and 7 the écusson may be drawn out in a cusped point over the blade.

The four styles peculiar to swords of Group II are inevitably very similar in appearance to some of the preceding ones, but there are distinct differences which set them clearly apart, so they must be classified separately.

Fig. 97. From "The Lives of the Two Offas", Matthew Paris, c. 1250.

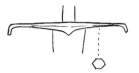

Style 8.

Style 8.   This might be compared with 4, but it is quite distinctively different. Its section is hexagonal; generally sharp and well-defined, but in poor specimens somewhat blurred. The arms are generally straight, though there are curved examples (plate 23), and the écusson is very solid and grows, as it were, naturally out of the two arms, which taper gradually outward to sharply downturned tips (plate 32)[9].

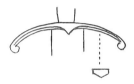

Style 9.

Style 9.   Akin to 7 in that it is ribbon-like in section, but the resemblance ends there. The ends are always rolled over, in section it is either flat on top and V-shaped underneath or of flat diamond section, and the ecusson grows naturally to a cusp from the slight taper of the arms (plate 22C, and figs. 74 and 75). Many are shown on English brasses between 1390–1440.[10]

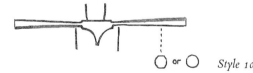

Style 10.

Style 10.   Like 2, but the arms, long and slender, taper evenly *inwards* from the tips to the very sharply defined and "built-up" écusson. The section may be circular, square or octagonal (plates 25 and 46D).

---

[9] There is a group of swords, almost identical in form and size, of which plate 27A is an example. Others are in the collections of the Society of Antiquaries, the late Sir James Mann, the Musée de l'Armée in Paris, the Guildhall in London, of Mr. C. O. von Kienbusch in New York, and Mr. E. A. Christensen of Copenhagen, and Mr. Eric Valentine.

[10] See note 5.

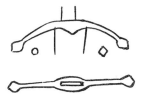

Style 11.

Style 11. May be long or short, curved or straight. Characteristic are knobbed ends and a circular or rhomboidal section (fig. 104, plates 36A, 37, 43B and 44C).

Style 12.

Style 12. The arms are strongly curved in the horizontal plane; the cross makes a flattened S shape when seen in plan (plates 41, 43D). On the evidence of the large number of swords furnished with this style of cross (generally mounted with pommels of Type Z) in the Arsenal at Venice, it seems reasonable to suppose that it, like the Type Z pommels, was of a Venetian fashion. Many of these "Venetian" hilts have been found in Hungary.

While we may suppose that this horizontal curvature of the cross was adopted to provide a measure of extra protection for the hand, we can be in no doubt that the various additional guards added to the cross were for this purpose and no other. First datable in the mid-14th century these extra guards took the form of rings added to the cross, either below it on one side (plate 39B) or on both (plate 39C) in the same plane as the blade; at its side, spanning the écusson at right-angles to the plane of the blade, or springing from one side of the upper edge of the cross and arching toward the pommel, as a guard for the knuckles. These four dispositions of the ring were used singly or together.

The finger-ring seems to have been the earliest. An example of perhaps

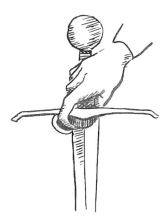

Fig. 98. From a painting in the museum at Valencia, c. 1443.

118

1325 is a back-edged sword (plate 43A) in Rome of a pattern distinctive of the years between 1275 and 1325, its blade inlaid with marks suggesting the same dating. Better known is the sword of Type XIX in the Armouries of the Tower of London (plate 39B) dated positively to the year 1432 by the Arabic inscription on its blade.[11] This date is of course a terminus ante quem; it may well have been made before 1400. A sword in a painting of St. Martin in the Valencia Museum, of *c.* 1443 (fig. 98) has a ring, but the earliest datable example in art is in a Crucifixion by "The Master of the Codex of St. George", a Sienese artist

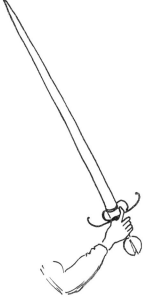

Fig. 99. Sword with fully developed hilt in a drawing by Martin Schongraner, c. 1475.

who painted it between 1340 and 1350. This is in the cloisters of the Metropolitan Museum of Art, New York (No. 61.100.1.2).

An early example of the double ring is on a wall-painting at Mondoneda of about 1440.[12] This double ring of the form known to collectors as "pas d'âne", (another example of the incorrect usage so dear to 19th century connoisseurs)[13] seems to have had its origin in the Peninsula. It is shown in the art of Spain and Portugal before it appears in Italian painting. Nuño Gonçalves, the Portuguese artist, painted as early as 1460 swords which correspond exactly to existing specimens, for instance the swords of Gonsalvo de Cordova and Ferdinand the Catholic in the Armeria Real at Madrid.[14] Hilts of an even more developed character, with "pas d'âne" and two side-rings (one on the cross and one joining the lower extremities of the two branches) may be seen on the great

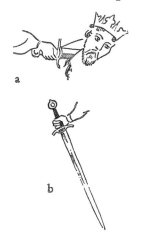

Fig. 100. Swords with side-ring, c. 1425.

[11] Chap. 11, p. 73. Combe and de Cosson, op. cit.

[12] Demmin, *Arms and Armour*, p. 190.

[13] In the 18th century this term "pas d'âne" was applied to the double shells of a small-sword. The double rings below the cross ("quillons" in 18th century terminology) were, appropriately, called the "branches".

[14] Chap. 11, p. 74. Cf. plates 38, 39C.

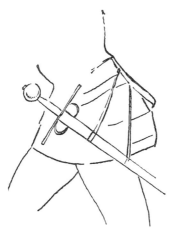

Fig. 101. From "The Conversion of St. Paul" by Luca Signorelli, Loreto. Before 1484.

"Arzila" tapestries of Pastraña, c. 1475.[15] Though this type of hilt does not often appear in German art, a drawing of c. 1475 by Martin Schongrauer (fig. 99) shows one.

The single side-ring is seldom shown in art—perhaps because most swords are presented to the spectator full-face, as it were, in paintings—though there are a few examples. One is clearly shown in a Spanish Bible illustrated between 1422 and 1433 (fig. 100a), and another (fig. 100b) in a Bohemian MS. of the same period (1420). Existing examples are rare. There is one (c. 1450) in the Armeria Real at Madrid[16] and another which used to be in my possession (plate 43B.) of c. 1425.[17]

In Italian painting after c. 1475 the fully developed hilt is common. Many, which if they turned up in the sale-room today would be dated c. 1550 or a little later, are shown in paintings datable to the 1470's; e.g. in the hand of a St. Michael by Pinturiccio, done between 1473 and 1481 (fig. 102).

The length of a sword's cross was probably determined partly by personal fancy and partly by the need to balance the blade properly. Thus, if a cross is very long (say above 9″) it must be slender or it will over-weight the hilt, and if it is very short (say below 5″) then it should be stout, or it will underweight the hilt. There are exceptions to the latter rule (plate 5C is a case in point) but very rarely to the former.

The cross of the ordinary fighting sword is rarely decorated, but when it is the adornment is of the most restrained kind. It is curious to reflect how completely different the everyday "knightly" sword of the period following the years around 1050 is from its Viking, Frankish and Anglo-Saxon predecessors upon which so much elaborate decorative effort was lavished. Only in exceptional cases do swords dating before c. 1250 seem to have any decoration

[15] Mann, Sir James, Archaeologia LXXXIII, "Armour worn in Spain from the 10th to the 15th centuries", plate LXXXV.

[16] Cat. Hist.-Descriptivo. No. G.30.

[17] The Archaeology of Weapons, pp. 330–31, plate 20b. Coll, David Drey,

on their crosses, though simply enriched pommels are fairly common. However, there are two swords, one of undoubted English provenance and one of possible English make, which have their crosses decorated with engraved patterns exactly similar in style to English manuscript paintings of the years between *c.* 1230– 1300. The first is the so-called "Conyers Falchion" preserved in the library of Durham Cathedral.[18]

Fig. 102. St. Michael, by Pin-turiccio. Leipzig, between 1473–1481.

Though this is a falchion and not a straight two-edged sword and so is outside the scope of this book, its hilt is typical of any 13th century sword (fig. 94). The decoration of its cross includes little "Worms" (dragons and wyverns) tucked into the ends, with a running pattern of leaves and tendrils joining the extremities (fig. 103). The other, a sword of no known provenance, is even more typically English in its decoration—which is only upon the cross, unlike the Conyers Falchion whose pommel bears on one side the leopards of England and on the other the eagle of the Empire, each shield being framed in running tendrils as on the cross. This second

Fig. 103. Decoration upon the arms of the cross of the Conyers Falchion.

sword (in a private collection in London)[19] has a cross of Style 5, in each end of which is a little "Babewyn", so typical of English manuscript decoration; a grotesque face in profile with no body, and tiny legs coming out of its neck.[20]

A popular form of embellishment after *c.* 1225 is one or more incised lines girdling the ends of the cross about a quarter of an

[18] Fully described in *The Archaeology of Weapons*, op. cit., p. 236–7, fig. 117; illustrated in Laking, op. cit., I, p. 128–9, figs. 157, 158.

[19] The collection of Mrs. How.

[20] Oakeshott, W. F. *The Sequence of English Medieval Art*, 1950,

Fig. 104. Sword, c. 1450, from the Dino Collection. Metropolitan Museum, New York.

inch from the extremity—this only on crosses of Styles 1a and 2. In the early 15th century this became popular again, on crosses of 1a, 2, 10 and 11. In these cases the lines are often in the form of chevrons, often accompanied by a group of radiating lines similarly engraved on the écusson—a decorative feature found by itself in most of those cross-styles which have a cusped écusson (plates 25 and 43B).

Throughout the period c. 1250–1350 the ends of crosses of Styles 5 and 6 may be adorned with indentations, one, two or more according to taste (plate 7). The knobbed form of cross (Style 11) may have its terminal knobs decorated or formed en suite with the pommel, as in a fine sword in the Dino Collection in the Metropolitan Museum in New York[21] (fig. 104). See also the swords shown in plates 36B and 43B. After c. 1450 the decoration of incised lines on the cross seems to have become less popular, though the various forms of fluting or similar adornment on the écusson remained in vogue (plate 41), varied by an occasional ovoid boss in very low relief[22] (figs. 76, 78 and plate 44C).

There are two exceptional swords, one in the Danish National Museum at Copenhagen,[23] and the other in a private collection[24] in London. Both have crosses each end of which is carved into a beast's head, very reminiscent of similar decorative motifs of the Migration and Viking periods. The sword in private hands is incomparably the finer and more important. Its cross is of Style 4, and the little heads on its downturned ends are of the most masterly workmanship (plates 3A and 4B). The Copenhagen sword (see p. 64) has a straight and very short cross of Style 2, with heads far more crudely executed (plate 28B).

[21] See Laking, op. cit., 1, p. 289, fig. 670A.

[22] This form of decoration appears on many English crosses of the first half of the 15th century, e.g. Sir T. Braunstone, Wisbech, Cambs., 1401; Sir Richard Fox, Arkesden, Essex, 1439; Sir Robert Del Botho, Wilmslow, Cheshire, 1460.

[23] Cat. No. R. 29.

[24] Mr. Mark Dinely. See also *The Archaeology of Weapons*, op. cit., pp. 213–215. These heads are identical in form and style with those carved on the N. porch of Southwell Minster.

The classic example of a medieval sword with its cross-ends decorated with beasts is of course the Sword of Charlemagne in the Louvre in Paris. There are two schools of thought about this sword; one school[25] regards it as being of 13th century workmanship, style and design, while the other[26] allows it to be of the period assigned to it by tradition of its use.

Why a hilt of a form so typical of the 9th century, with decoration even more characteristic of that age, should be confidently placed four centuries too late is extraordinarily hard to understand.

The cross is longer, certainly, than the average Viking or Frankish sword of that period, but there is plenty of evidence for crosses of more than 4″ in length.[27] The "Tea-Cosy" pommel is as common in 800 as it is rare in 1200, while the decorative style is quite alien to the later date. There is perhaps one reason why the later date is asserted: stamped below the cross, in letters and figures of a style consistent with a 13th century date, is a note of the weight of the gold of which the hilt is made. This however does not constitute proof that it was of necessity *made* then; in the course of centuries of use, care and cleaning, the hilt may have been taken apart and re-mounted several times. That such a re-mounting may have taken place in the 13th century, and the note of the weight of gold made on the cross, is entirely consistent with possibility— have we not the example of the "Sword of St. Maurice" in Vienna where a hilt was refurbished for Otto IV? An even closer instance is the known fact that the Charlemagne sword was dismounted, cleaned and furnished with a new grip for the coronation of Napoleon I.

There are a few such "parade" swords of the 13th and 14th centuries which have decorated crosses, i.e. the Vienna coronation "Sword of St. Maurice" where the cross (Style 1) of gilded iron is engraved with the phrase "Christus Vincit, Christus Reinat, Christus Inperat", the antiphon from the coronation anthem "Laudes Regiae". It was also the war-cry of the crusading Franks

[25] Laking, op. cit., vol. I, pp. 89–93, figs. 112, 114, 115; and Ada Bruhn Hoffmeyer, op. cit., pl. vii, vol. II, p. 9, who follows Laking.

[26] Mann, Sir James, Journal of the Royal Society of Arts, "The influence of Art on Instruments of War", 1941, vol. LXXXIX, no. 4599, p. 749.

[27] Petersen, op. cit., and *The Sword in Anglo-Saxon England*, op. cit., figures from 9th–10th century Anglo-Saxon MSS. (B.M.MS. Cott., Nero C. IV, Nero C. VI) and the Utrecht Psalter, *c*. 850 (figs. 108, 109, 112).

in the third crusade,[28] but this latter fact does not seem so relevant to the decoration of a weapon used solely in coronation ceremonies as the former.

In the Armeria Real at Madrid there is a magnificent and well-known sword attributed to the ownership of Ferdinand III (St. Ferdinand) of Castile (1223–1253) (see fig. 64, p. 96 above). Its cross is most elaborate, each end curling round completely to enclose a little trefoil ornament. The arms and ecusson are decorated with a typically 13th century engraved pattern of tendrils and leaves.[29]

Also in Spain is another little-known sword attributed to St. Ferdinand. It is kept in the treasury of the Cathedral of Seville, in the nature of a relic (the point is embedded in a gold mount, and the sword stands in the manner of a cross). The cross of Style 1 is made, too delicately for use, from lengths of red cornelian set in small mounts of silver-gilt embellished with mudejar ornament. The grip is similarly made, and the pommel (Type I) is of rock-crystal.[30] The hilt of the famous sword of Sancho IV of Castile (before 1295) is decorated with similar mudejar ornament, incorporating cufic characters, which, though hardly subject to interpretation, do contain the word "Allah".[31] This sword, in spite of its elaborately ornamented hilt, is no sword of ceremony, but a good, practical, fighting weapon. (See p. 37 above and plates 7 and 9).

There are a few other practical swords with decorated crosses. A splendidly preserved sword of Type XII in the Instituto del Conde de Valencia de Don Juan in Madrid[32] has a Style 6 cross of bronze-gilt with the words "Dios es Vencedor en Todo. Dios es

[28] Roger of Hoveden.

[29] "Catalogo Historico Descriptivo", op. cit., No. G.22.

[30] Mann, J. G., "Some Notes on the Armour worn in Spain from the 10th to the 15th Centuries", Archaeologia, vol. XIII, p. 303, plate XCI, 1; and Leguina, E., *Espadas Historicos*, 1898, pp. 75–117.

[31] This information was given me by the late Professor Storm Rice, unfortunately only verbally, shortly before his tragic death in 1962.

[32] Catalogue of the Exhibition of Spanish Royal Armour held in the Tower of London, 1959, no. 26, p. 19 and plate XIIIa; Laking, op. cit., vol. I, p. 133, fig. 166; and Sir James Mann, "Some Notes on the Armour Worn in Spain from the 10th to the 15th Centuries", Archaeologia, vol. XIII, 1932, p. 305 and plate XCI, 3. It came from San Vicente near Logroño, and is held to have miraculous properties. Sometimes called the sword of Santa Casilda.

Fig. 105. Sword of Frederic III, c. 1470, Musée de Cluny.

Vencedor en Todo A" in low relief (plate 18). In the Metropolitan Museum of Art in New York that most magnificent
sword of Type XIV (p. 53 and plate 15) has a very Viking-like
ornament of silver wires set vertically into its delicately shaped
cross of Style 4. Another fine sword (present location unknown)
which used to be in the Richard Zischille Collection[33] has a Style 6
cross engraved with the words, "Dextera Domine Facit Virtu-

---

[33] Forrer, Robert, *Der Waffensammlung von Herrn Richard Zischille*, 1893.

tem" on one side and "Dexter Domine Exala Vit Me" on the other.

In the 15th century decorated crosses were more common—or more have survived. Sometimes the decoration was of the simple engraved or incised lines as described above, but some swords, particularly those of ceremony called "bearing swords", have elaborately adorned crosses. A sword in the Waffensammlung of the Kunsthistorisches Museum in Vienna,[34] made in 1438 for the Emperor Sigismund I, has its cross modelled in the form of a "Worm" (plate 42B), the emblem of the "Gesellschaft der Lind-wurms" of which society Sigismund was a member. The sword of Frederick of Saxony made c. 1424–25 has a "crabstock" cross twisted and knobbed like a twiggy length of stick, like the Ragged Staff device of the Earls of Warwick.[35] The bearing sword of Frederic III, made in 1440, has a cross formed in a manner similar to the sword of St. Ferdinand at Seville, only the material is horn and gilt copper instead of cornelian and silver-gilt[36] (plate 42A). This hilt, so elaborately decorated, is in sharp contrast to the same emperor's war sword preserved in the Musée de Cluny (fig. 106), where the Style 6 cross is simply decorated with horizontal lines of roping and vertical ridges on the outside only.

Fig. 107. Sword No. A467, Wallace Collection.

Many late 15th century swords with Style 5 and 6 crosses have ribs running longitudinally along the middle of the arms (plate 38). These may be roped or plain and only appear on one side of the cross. Many crosses of this style have the arms recurved horizontally with the ends curled sharply. Some are plain while some have the curled ends roped. Where the ends are plain, as in the sword in the Bayerische National Museum shown in plate 45, sometimes the earlier practice of decorating the cross with a

[34] Cat. No. A 49, 5A, Jahrbuch der Kunsthistorischen Sammlung in Wien, Band 57.1, 1961; Ortwin Gamber, Die Mittelalterlichen Blankwaffen der Wiener Waffen-sammlung, p. 24–5, abb. 14.

[35] Z.H.W.K., vol. I, p. 81; and Bruhn Hoffmeyer, plate XXVIa and p. 30, no. 73.

[36] See note 27, Gamber, op. cit., p. 25–6, abb. 15.

pair of incised lines girdling the extremity is used.

The practice of recurving the arms of the cross horizontally is of greater antiquity than is generally allowed. For instance, we find it clearly shown in (a) a manuscript of c. 1425, "The Hours of Elizabeth the Queene", formerly in the collection of C. W. Dyson Perrins (fig. 106); and (b) in a Spanish Bible of c. 1425.[37] In the University Museum of Ethnology and Archaeology at Cambridge is a sword of Type XX,[38] with a blade similar to the sword of the same type in Toronto (plate 39A) and a hilt similar to the one shown in the Dyson Perrins manuscript which is unlikely to date later than c. 1430–40. There is a fine sword in the Wallace Collection in

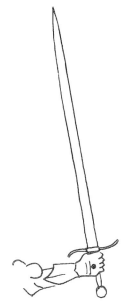

Fig. 108. From a drawing by Martin Schöngrauer, c. 1475.

London (no. A467) which in the catalogue[39] is dated c. 1500–1520 (fig. 107), yet which is identical in appearance and form with a sword in a drawing by Martin Schongrauer of 1475 (fig. 108).

This chapter does not by any means profess to catalogue all the decorated crosses which survive. There are many, most of which have been adequately described and illustrated elsewhere; but there are the crosses which show distinct national characteristics which have not been dealt with. In Denmark, during the 15th century, an exaggerated form of Style 6, very sharply arched, seems to be peculiar to that nation;[40] while in Spain crosses of the same style exhibit a form of pierced ornament (plate 43C) which seems characteristic of Spanish practice,[41] though a similar

[37] Casa de Alba. Rabi More Arreguel de Guadalajara (The Roxburgh Club published a facsimile in 1920–22).

[38] No. 32, 243.

[39] Wallace Collection Catalogues, Arms and Armour 1962. No. A467, p. 244.

[40] Bruhn Hoffmeyer, op. cit., plates XXXIV, XXXV, XXXVIII.

[41] There is a late 15th-century example in the Armeria Real in Madrid; and slightly earlier ones in the collection of the late Georges Pauilhac of Paris and of Mr. Mark Dinely in London. (Gay, V., Glossaire Arch. Vol. II, p. 282.)

decorated cross of Style 5, in the Bayerische National Museum at Munich, seems to be of German origin.[42]

In this country there is a group of swords with crosses all showing the same characteristics. They are of Style 6, and each has a perforated cross, which looks like a quatrefoil, at either end of the cross. Two of these are in the City Museum at Lincoln. One is on the very ugly Type XVI sword (plate 26A); the other is now missing, but in a drawing made in 1854 it is clearly shown on the blade, which still remains in the museum. A third cross of this kind is in the Castle Museum at Norwich (plate 26B) on a falchion found at Thorpe. There is a fourth sword, not similar in type to the two Lincoln ones (which are XVI's) in the Wallace Collection. This is a XV, but its cross (of Style 5) still has the perforated crosses. There is a brass, too, at Gorleston in Suffolk dating about 1325 which shows a cross precisely similar to the two at Lincoln and the one at Norwich. It is tempting to think that this may be an English style, for the Wallace Collection sword is from the Nieuwerkerke Collection and was found in France, so could easily be of English origin. One might even risk the temptation to go farther, and suggest a local East Anglian style, for all these swords were found in Norfolk and the brass is in Suffolk.

[42] Bruhn Hoffmeyer, plate XXIIb. A reproduction of this sword may be seen in the Armouries of the Tower of London, attached to the figure in German Gothic armour mounted on the horse armour of the Duke of Anhalt Zerbst, Waldemar IV, 1473–1508.

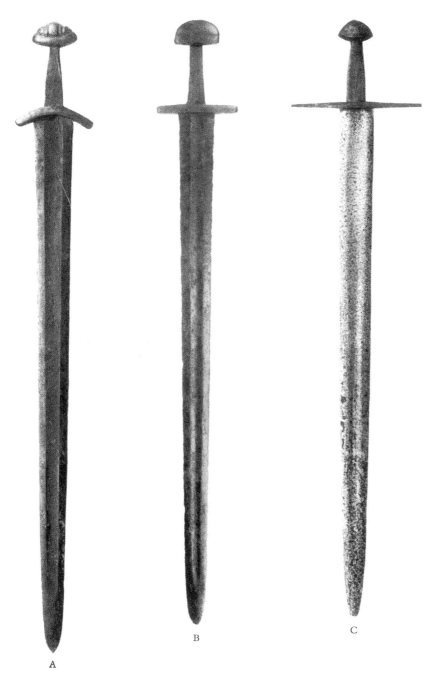

1. A. Viking sword of Wheeler's Type VII; *c.* 900. Found in the River Witham near Lincoln. The blade inlaid in iron (LEULFRIL). B. Viking sword, *c.* 950; Type VIIIb. Found in the Scheldt. The iron inlay in the blade has not so far been examined and deciphered. C. Type VIII; *c.* 950. The hilt and blade of this sword could equally well belong to Type X, but the iron inlays, INGELRII on one side and a non-Christian symbolic design on the other, suggest the earlier type; see fig. 7.

A B C

2. Type X. A. This sword might date from the mid-10th century, but the inscription on its blade suggests the second half of the 11th century. (See fig. 127, p. 140.) B. Early 12th century (or late 11th?). The grip, bound with silver wire finished at top and bottom with fillets of silver decorated with a row of punched circles, appears to be original. C. Second half of the 10th century. Blade inscribed in iron letters (CONSTAININUS on one side and INONINEDNI on the other).

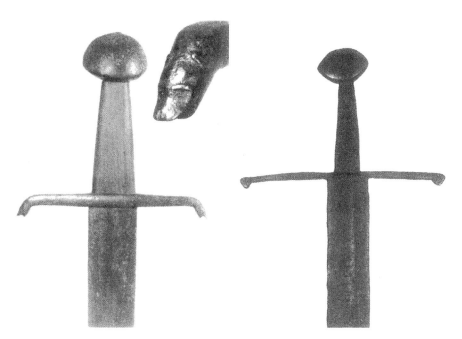

3. A. Type XI (see plate 4B). Inset, detail of small beast's head on the ends of the cross.

3. B. Type XI. Style 4 cross with rather unusual knobbed ends.

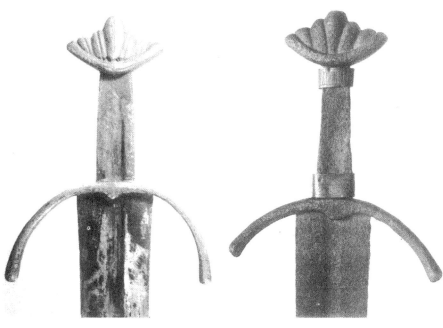

3. C. Type XII (plate 8B). Pommel of Viking style, cross similar to many shown in 10th century Anglo-Saxon MS. pictures (i.e. B. M. Nero c. VI). Blade of fine form inlaid (in pewter) with inscriptions which clearly seem to be of 13th century date. Much of the original plating of pewter remains on the hilt. Found at Cawood in the River Ouse, Yorkshire.

3. D. Type XII. Found in a stone coffin at Korsoygaden, near Oslo. Hilt similar to 3C. No inscription on blade, but a clear runic one on the upper bronze fillet of the grip. "AVMVTÆR: GEÞE: MIK: AOSLIKÆR: AMK." The runes could be as late as c. 1300, and the style of the sword suggests a 13th century date rather than a 10th–11th century one.

4. Type XI. A. ?10th century with runic inscription incised in tang; another inlaid in the blade. B. Early 12th century. GICELINMEFECIT inlaid in iron. C. Second half of the 11th century or first half of 12th. Latten inlays in blade (see fig. 131, p. 142). D. Mid-12th century.

5. A. Type XIa. Second half of the 12th century. Blade inscribed in tiny letters oso. B. Type XI. The "Sword of St. Maurice" in Vienna. Coronation sword of the Empire. Hilt may be c. 1200, fitted for the coronation of Otto IV or may be contemporary with the blade (cf. the sword on plate 4C) simply re-gilded and engraved for that occasion. C. Type XIa. Second half of the 12th century.

A   C

B

6. Type XII. A. Hilt form suggests an early date, c. 1200. The blade has a strong and well defined ricasso about 2″ long. B. Second half of the 13th century. Found in Whittlesey Mere, Cambridgeshire. For detail of inscription, see plate 48C. C. Second half of the 13th century. The blade has a double fuller. Found near Lincoln in the River Witham.

7. Type XII, I, 6. Spanish, before 1295. From the tomb of Sancho IV (el Bravo) of Castile, +1295. The cross and pommel of ?latten ?bronze are decorated with elaborate mudejar ornament, incorporating Cufic characters which have so far defied elucidation, except that the word "Allah" occurs on the cross. The grip, of a dark red-brown wood, has on either side three circular panels, the arms of Castile quartered with Leon, painted in glass, flanked by small panels of similar technique, chequy or and sable. The three main panels are now all missing from one side.

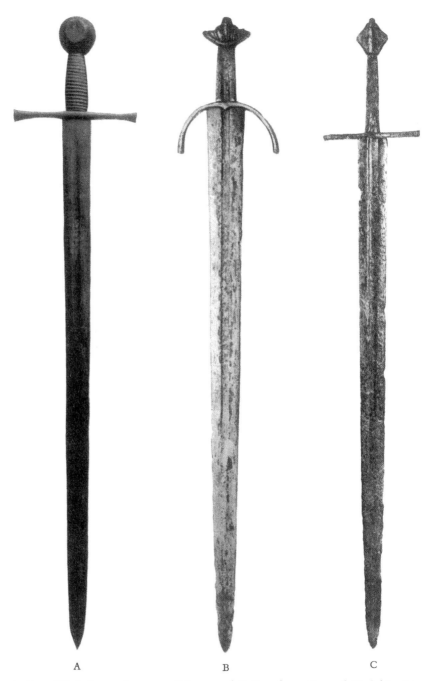

A B C

8. Type XII. A. Late 13th century. Grip restored. B. Found near Cawood, Yorkshire. Late 13th century (see plate 3C). C. Found near Cambridge. The grip is unusually long for a sword of this type; corrosion near the tip of the blade may have narrowed it to the proportion of a XII, whereas in its original complete form it may have been a XIII.

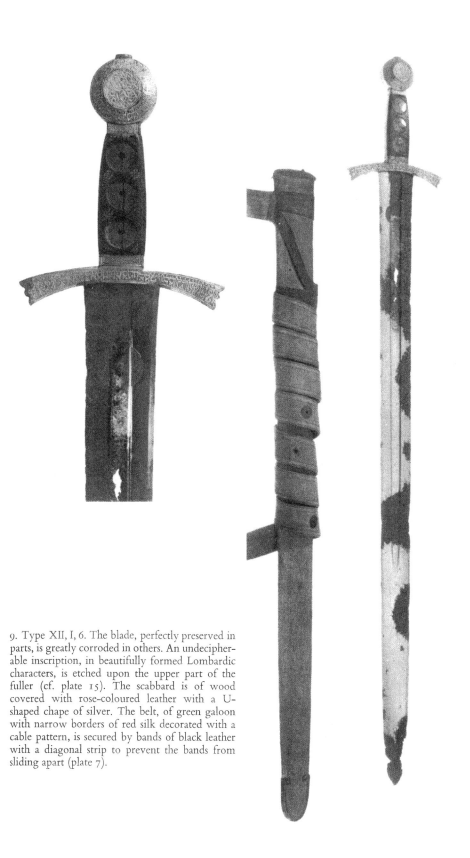

9. Type XII, I, 6. The blade, perfectly preserved in parts, is greatly corroded in others. An undecipherable inscription, in beautifully formed Lombardic characters, is etched upon the upper part of the fuller (cf. plate 15). The scabbard is of wood covered with rose-coloured leather with a U-shaped chape of silver. The belt, of green galoon with narrow borders of red silk decorated with a cable pattern, is secured by bands of black leather with a diagonal strip to prevent the bands from sliding apart (plate 7).

10. Type XII, H, ?2. Found in the coffin of Fernando de la Cerda, a son of Alfonso X of Castile, +1270. The grip is bound with yellow silk cord, elaborately knotted up the centre line of each face, with an equally elaborate overbinding of thicker red silk cord. The tassel at the top is also of red silk as are the remains of a similar tassel at the bottom. The bronze pommel has been turned to a bright blue-green colour from the effect of the prince's hand, which has also caused the cross of iron to decompose considerably. The scabbard is perfectly preserved with its belt-fittings of buckskin; but both sections of the belt have been cut off (cf. the sculptured scabbards and belts shown in figs. 16, 17, 118).

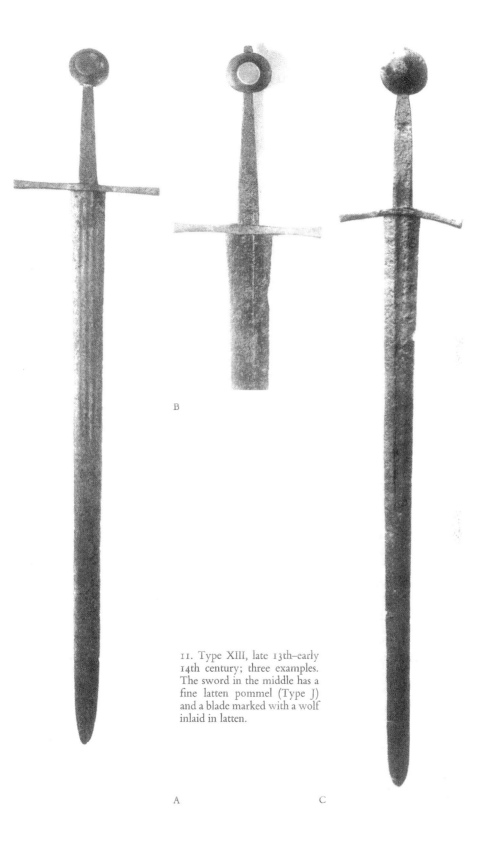

B

11. Type XIII, late 13th–early 14th century; three examples. The sword in the middle has a fine latten pommel (Type J) and a blade marked with a wolf inlaid in latten.

A   C

12. Type XIIIb. Late 13th, early 14th century.

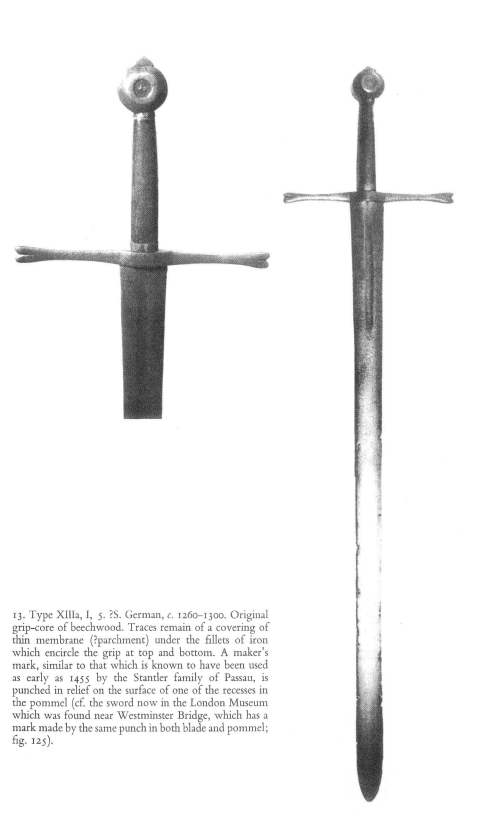

13. Type XIIIa, I, 5. ?S. German, *c.* 1260–1300. Original
grip-core of beechwood. Traces remain of a covering of
thin membrane (?parchment) under the fillets of iron
which encircle the grip at top and bottom. A maker's
mark, similar to that which is known to have been used
as early as 1455 by the Stantler family of Passau, is
punched in relief on the surface of one of the recesses in
the pommel (cf. the sword now in the London Museum
which was found near Westminster Bridge, which has a
mark made by the same punch in both blade and pommel;
fig. 125).

A   B   C

14. A. Type XIIIa; *c.* 1280–1310. B. Type XIIIa. The blade of fine quality, inlaid A.C.L.I. and a mark of a bell within a shield. The original leather-bound grip survives. C. Type XVa. Second half of the 14th century. Compared with preceding types, showing completely different type of blade, though hilt is similar in proportions and akin in shape.

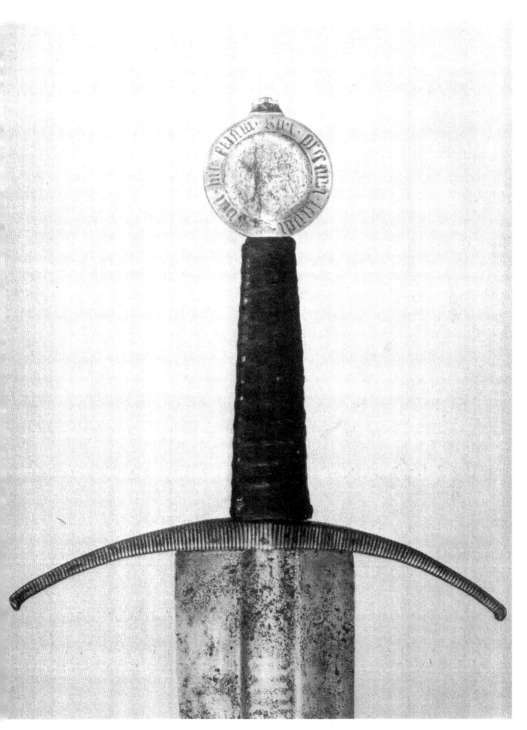

15. Type XIV, J1, 4. ?Italian, first quarter of the 14th century (see next page).

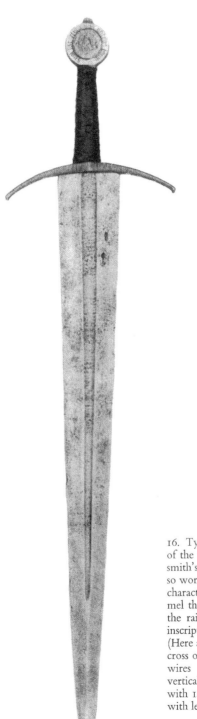

16. Type XIV, J1, 4. ?Italian, first quarter of the 14th century. The broad blade bears a smith's mark and an etched inscription, now so worn as to be illegible, in Gothic miniscule characters. On either face of the bronze pommel there is a flat ring of silver surrounding the raised central panel, with the engraved inscription *Sunt hic etiam sua praecuna laudi* (Here also are the Heralds of His praise). The cross of bronze is delicately inlaid with silver wires closely spaced encircling the cross vertically. The grip is of wood, bound about with 14 rings of cord or thong, and covered with leather.

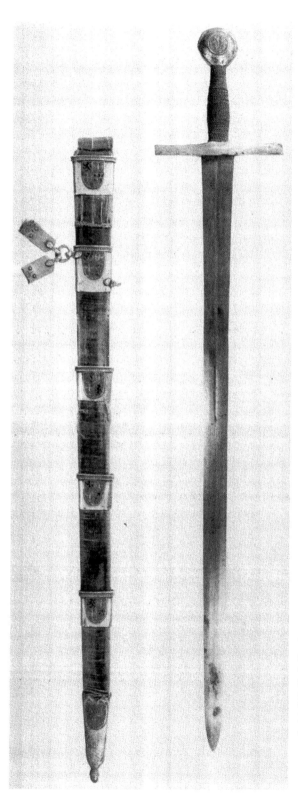

17. Type XIIIb, I, 2. Spanish, before 1319. A small weapon made for a boy. The arms, contained in enamelled panels in the pommel and in the six silver mounts of the scabbard, are the same as are used on the seal of one of the sons of Alfonso X (el Sabio) of Castile—Don Juan, el de Tarifa, who was killed fighting against the Moors in 1319. The cross and pommel are of iron plated with silver-gilt, and the grip is bound with twisted silver wire. The scabbard, of wood covered with red velvet, is fitted with chape and locket of silver, with four additional silver mounts between. The silver belt ends and rings remain, but have been incorrectly re-set together on one ring of the locket. On the back of the uppermost mount is a silver-mark, a shield, with two crossed keys surmounting a star impaled with two unidentifiable marks. The keys and star were used, with the star above the keys, by Pope Gregory X on his coinage in the 15th century.

18. Hilt of "Santa Casilda" sword (plate 19C) XII, G, 6. Gilded iron. The pommel is decorated in relief round the border with an inscription in Lombardic capitals AVE. MARIA. GRATIA. PLENA. enclosing the arms Barry Wavy, argent and gules. The cross is similarly decorated with the words DIOS. ES. VINCENDOR. EN. TOD/O. DIOS. ES. VENCENDOR. EN. TODO. Grip bound with red leather, with trellised overbinding of flat thongs secured by gilt-headed pins.

19. Three types, all in use 1250–1325, contrasted. A. Type XIIIb; *c.* 1300. B. Type XIV; *c.* 1300. C. Type XII; *c.* 1250–1300.

A

B

C

20. A. Type XIV. Early 14th century. Well-formed pommel of Type W. Grip restored.
Marked in the blade on either face is an unusual inscription. The letters IOIO (or TOTO),
each repeated twice, in the manner of the lettering round the edge of a coin, to form a circle.
B. Type XVI. First half of the 14th century. For inscription on blade, see fig. 32, p. 62.
C. Type XIV (or XVI?). The corrosion of the point end of the blade makes it hard to
classify. There is an almost identical sword, of Type XVI, in the City Museum at Lincoln.

21. Hilt of the Monza sword (plate 22B). The pommel is inlaid with four silver shields engraved alternately with the Viper of Visconti and the Cross of Milan. Set under the riveted end of the tang are two silver washers, the large lower one rosette-shaped with ribs and points following the ribs on the pommel, the upper, smaller one circular and knurled. The grip is of oval section, bound with twisted copper wire with traces of gilding. Fitted over the tang between the grip and the cross is a silver chappe decorated in low relief with a double spray of foliage involving four-petalled flowers on a hatched ground within a border formed as a plaited tress of hair ending in a tassel at each side of the base of the grip. The other half is broken off; it is recorded as recently as 1915 that the sword bore the initials H·V (Hestor Viscomes). There is no trace of them anywhere else on the sword, so it seems that they were upon the lost half of the chappe. The tress suggests that Estore was a member of The Fellowship of the Tress (Zopfgesellschaft), a knightly association founded by the Archduke Albrecht I of Austria (1365–95).

A   B   C

22. A. Type XV. Late 13th–early 14th century. An identical sword is shown on the alabaster effigy (*c.* 1310) of Sir John de Hanbury, at Hanbury, Staffordshire. B. Type XV. Early 15th century sword of Estore Visconti. C. Type XVIII. Mid-15th century. An almost identical hilt is in the Musée de l'Armée in Paris. The sword as a whole is similar to the one attributed to Henry V in Westminster Abbey.

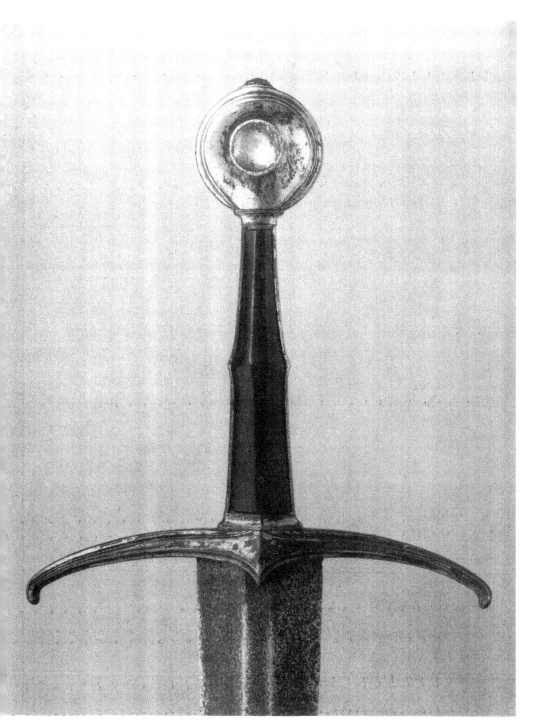

23. Hilt of plate 24. Pommel and cross are of bronze-gilt; the grip of horn is finished at top and bottom with fillets and supported up each side with strips of bronze-gilt.

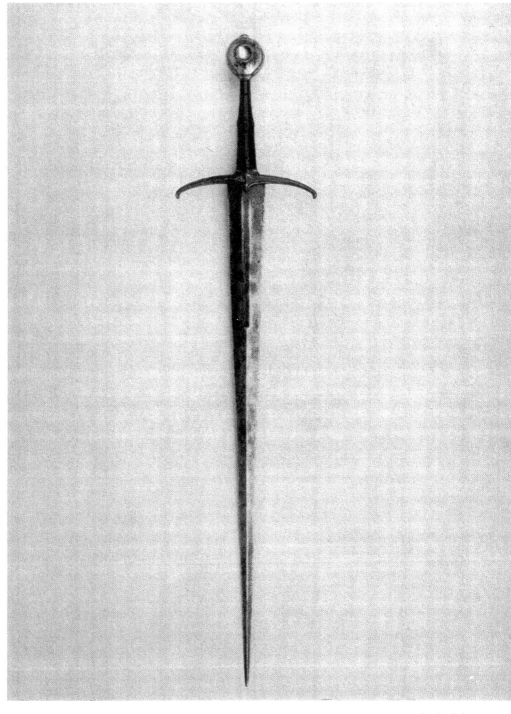

24. Type XV, J, 8 (curved). ?Italian, first half of the 15th century. The upper third of the blade has the central rib flattened off. The grip is rather long (5¼″) in proportion to the blade (28½″) but the sword is not a XVa.

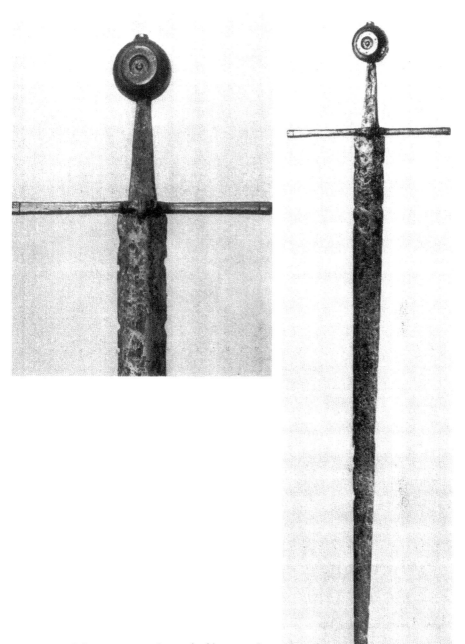

25. Type XV, J1, 10; *c.* 1400. Pommel of bronze. The cross is similar to that of the sword shown in the frontispiece and in plate 46D, though in this case it is heavier and not so slender. The blade is of a flat oval section rather than a flattened diamond section, but its outline is such that the sword should be regarded as of Type XV. Found in the River Ouse at Southery.

26. A. Type XVI, early 14th century. Style 6 cross with perforated ends and pommel of Type W. Found in the River Witham.

26. B. Falchion, early 14th century. Latten pommel crudely decorated, Type J. Cross similar to 27A. Found at Thorpe, Norwich.

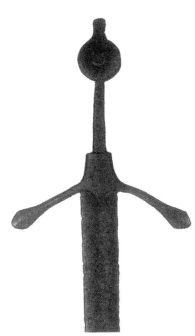

26. C. Type XV (see plate 27A); c. 1400. Possibly of English origin. Style 5 cross of similar character to 26A and 27A. There are recesses in the pommel for small shields of arms. Cf. plate 21.

26. D. Scottish sword, vaguely of Type XVIII. Identical in form with a sword on the grave-slab of Robert de Greenlaw in the churchyard of Kinkell, Aberdeenshire. He was killed at Harlaw in 1411, so this sword may date from c. 1400.

A   B   C

27. A. Type XV; *c.* 1400. The blade has a narrow fuller in its upper half. B. Type XV.
Second half of the 15th century. See plate 46D. C. Type XVa. Found in Lake Constance.

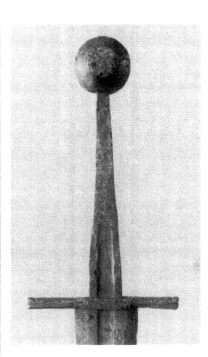

B

28. Type XVIa. First half of the 14th century. A. Found in London, now almost entirely destroyed by fire. The blade is marked in the fuller and on the tang with a punched fleur-de-lys in a shield. B. Blade similar to A, without reinforcement at the point. The ends of the cross are cut into small beasts' heads. C. This sword is of the same form and proportions as the well-known one of the same type in the Gwynn Collection (p. 48).

A   C

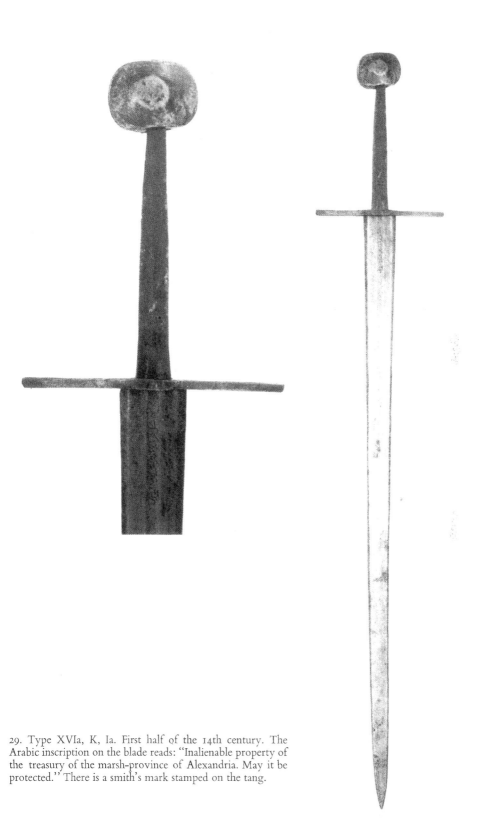

29. Type XVIa, K, Ia. First half of the 14th century. The Arabic inscription on the blade reads: "Inalienable property of the treasury of the marsh-province of Alexandria. May it be protected." There is a smith's mark stamped on the tang.

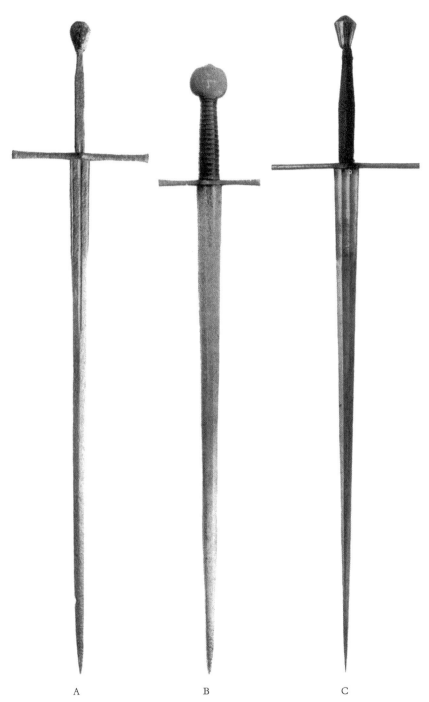

A   B   C

30. Type XVII. A. Second half of 14th century. The blade, with its long ricasso, is not of the true XVII section; it could be classified as of Type XVIIIa, but the ricasso seems mostly to be found on XVII's. B. Second half of the 14th century. The Arabic inscription gives the date 1424. Grip restored. C. Second half of the 14th century.

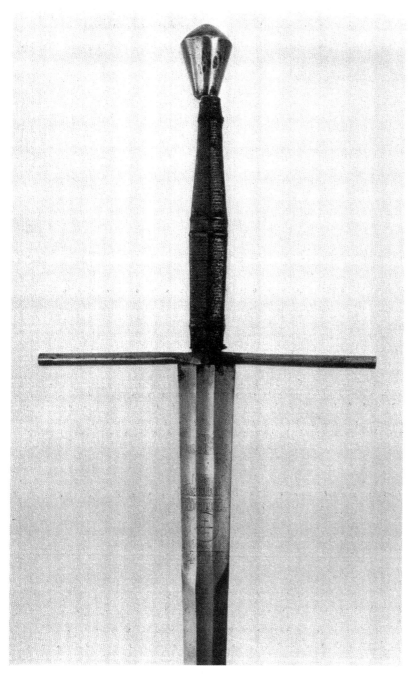

31. Hilt of plate 30C, XVII, T4, 1a. Until recently there was a leather chape, like the one on the sword in plate 47 in place at the bottom of the cord-bound, leather-covered grip. The inscription on the blade is fully dealt with by R. Wegeli, in *Z.H.W.K.* III, 3, p. 293.

32. Hilt of plate 34. The original grip is bound with fine leather over cord.

A

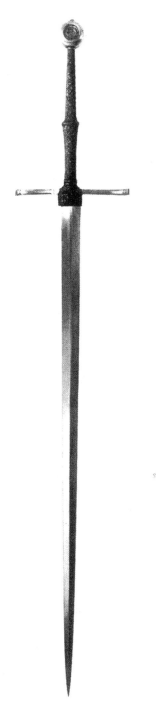

33. A. Type XVIIIb, T4, 4; *c.* 1400.
Typical of English effigies and brasses
between 1370–1425. B. Type XVIIIb,
J1, 12. German, second half of the
15th century. Typical of the swords
in the drawings of Dürer and
Schöngrauer.

B

34. Type XVIII, J, 8. First quarter of the 15th century.

A

B

35. A. Second half of the 14th century. The blade, though clean, is much worn. In its present shape it looks as if it belonged to Type XV, but before it was reduced by sharpening it may have been an XVIII. B. Late 15th century. Made in Milan for the Archduke Philip the Handsome. Grip and pommel are of ivory and bronze-gilt, cross of bronze-gilt; the upper part of the blade is etched and gilded.

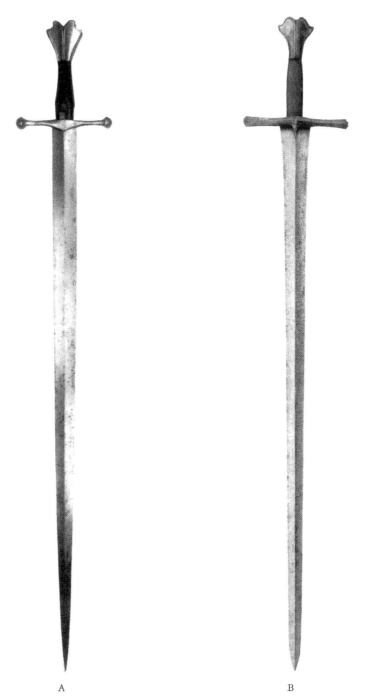

A   B

36. Type XVIIIa. A. ?Flemish, mid-15th century. The pommel (Type V) is of bronze-gilt, but the cross (Style 11) is of copper-gilt. The grip is of horn, most elegantly shaped to "grow" into the flower-like pommel. B. Mid-15th century. Hilt of gilded iron. The original leather-bound grip, much worn, had in the sword's lifetime been re-covered with a shaped grip, the shaped collars at top, bottom and centre having been formed under the covering of leather by fillets of wire. The sword was illustrated in *The Archaeology of Weapons*, plate 19C, with this grip still in position. It was removed by the Author in 1961.

37. Type XVIIIa, J, 11. Hilt of bronze gilt; the grip is bound with fine cord, with fillets of stouter cord at top, bottom and in the middle, covered with thin leather. The grip is short (4½″) in relation to the very big blade (35″).

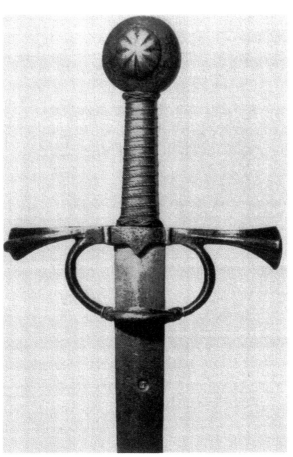

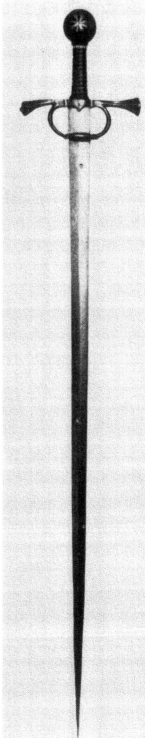

38. Type XVIIIc, G, 5+. Spanish, last quarter of the 15th
century. *Espada de Ropera*. The bladesmith's mark, a heraldic
stag trippant, is similar to that used by Meves Berns of
Solingen in the 17th century. The grip, of two sorts of wire
finished with turks' heads of wire at top and bottom, though
it has been used with the sword is probably a replacement, or a
re-binding, of early 16th century date.

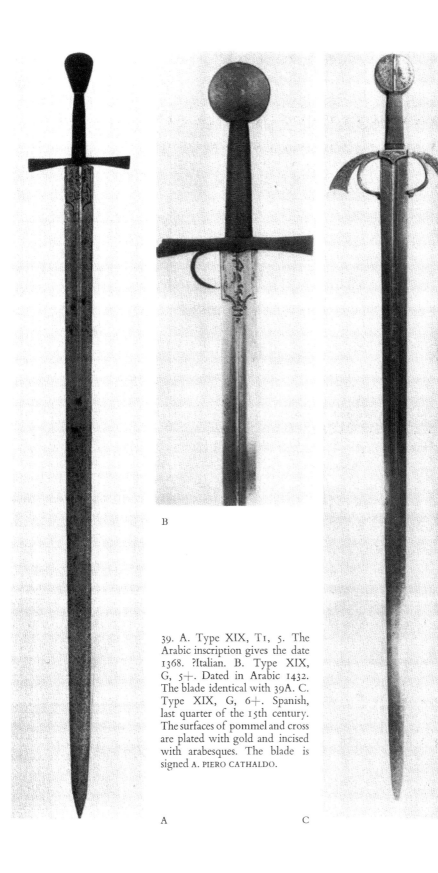

39. A. Type XIX, T1, 5. The Arabic inscription gives the date 1368. ?Italian. B. Type XIX, G, 5+. Dated in Arabic 1432. The blade identical with 39A. C. Type XIX, G, 6+. Spanish, last quarter of the 15th century. The surfaces of pommel and cross are plated with gold and incised with arabesques. The blade is signed A. PIERO CATHALDO.

B

A   C

A

B

C

40. Type XX. A. First quarter of the 14th century. A very large weapon, possibly a "Bearing Sword". B. First quarter of the 14th century. This Bearing Sword can be dated by reason of marks inlaid in the blade. C. An ordinary War Sword or Great Sword of the same type, mid-14th century, with an Arabic inscription dated 1427.

41. Venetian sword, second half of the 15th century, indefinite Type, pommel of Type Z, cross of Style 12 (see p. 111). From a castle on the River Piave. The grip has a spirally wound cord under the covering of leather.

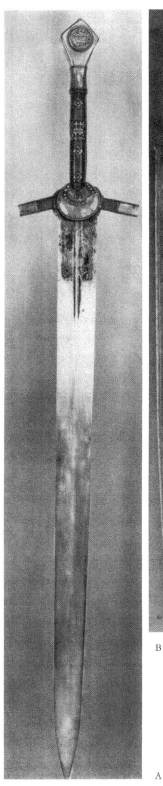

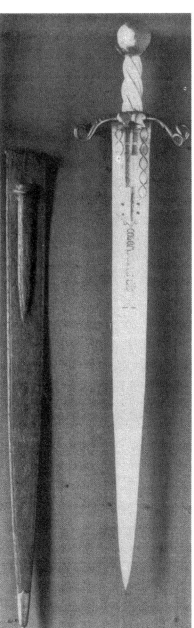

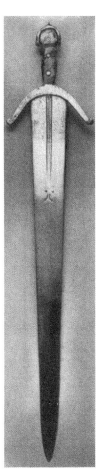

C

B

42. Type XX. A. Ceremonial sword of the Emperor Frederic III, *c.* 1450. B. Type XXa. Sword of the Emperor Sigismund I. made in 1435. The cross is made in the form of a dragon or "Worm", the emblem of the *Gesellschaft der Lindwurms* of which Sigismund was a member. C. Sword with a very crudely-made hilt of horn, in cinquedea form. This is so out of keeping with the magnificent quality of the blade that it seems to be a home-made replacement. (This photograph is not to scale with A and B: it is as large a weapon as B.)

A

43. A. Back-edged sword, early 14th century, with finger-ring.

43. B. XVIIIa, first quarter of the 15th century. Cross (Style 2) with side ring. "Hock-bottle" grip, bound with fine cord covered with ?doeskin dyed green.

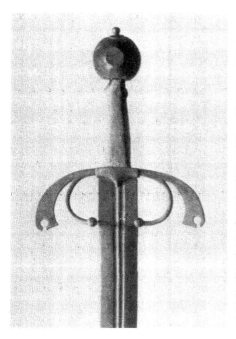

43. C. Type XIX. Spanish, last quarter of the 15th century. Developed ring-guards with small bars ending in knobs springing horizontally from the ends of the rings at right-angles to the plane of the blade.

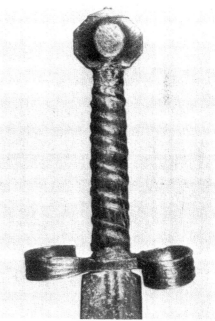

43. D. Indeterminate type, of "Venetian" fashion. Mid-15th century. Strongly curved cross of Style 12 associated with a normal pommel of Type I1.

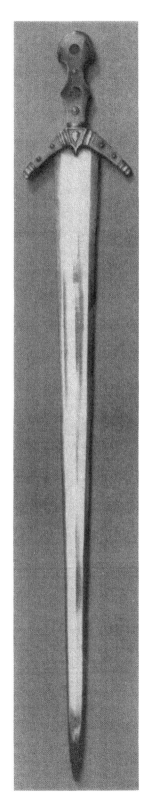

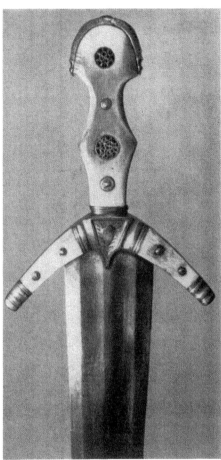

B

C

44. Type XX, late 15th century. A. Long blade ($31\frac{1}{2}''$) with cinquedea hilt. B. Hilt of A. Mammoth ivory mounted with bronze. C. Type XXa. Small sword, with hilt in the same class as the Borgia sword, possibly made for a boy and adapted to a man's use by cutting a piece out of the blade for the forefinger. Marked BA.

A

45. Hilt of plate 33B. Second half of the 15th century. Pommel and cross of bronze-gilt, grip (10½″ long) of tooled leather. Inset in the recess of the pommel is a gilt-bronze engraved plate showing the Virgin and Child. The circumference is inscribed in miniscule characters, O . MARIA . BIT . WIR . UNS.

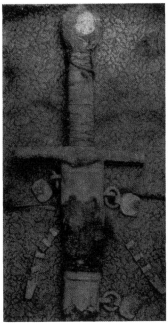

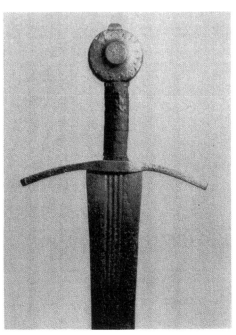

46. A. Type ?XIIIb, I, 2. Italian, early 14th century. Found in the coffin of Can Grande della Scala, +1329, Verona. Grip bound with silver wire with an overbinding of green silk. The scabbard, covered with red velvet, has two lockets and a chape of silver engraved with stylised floral patterns.

46. B. Type XIV, K, 1a (curved). ?Italian, early 14th century. Hilt of iron plated with silver. Grip covered with black leather bearing the impress of a diagonally wound thong or cord.

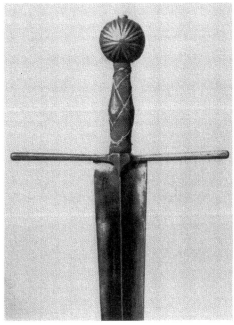

46. C. Type XVIIIa, ?V, ?2. German, mid-15th century. Hilt of bronze-gilt, grip of red wood bound with bronze-gilt fillets.

46. D. Type XV, G1, 10. Italian, mid-15th century. Grip covered with red velvet, bound with plain steel wire and twisted silver wire.

47. Type XVIa, K, 5. First half of the 14th century. Original grip of leather over cord with leather chape attached. The blade bears two marks: on one side a wild boar, on the other a unicorn. The chape is an elaborate double one, the under part consisting of a kind of cap to fit over the scabbard-mouth, the over part being the usual double flap (cf. plate 21); this is ornamented with punched dots.

48. Contrasting styles of inlay on blades. A. 10th century, sword of Type X. The letters are inlaid in iron; the surface of the blade surrounding them is plated with copper. B. First half of 10th century, Viking sword of Type VII found in the Thames. C. Second half of the 13th century, Type XII (plate 14B). Sword found in Whittlesey Mere, letters carefully made and inlaid in latten. D. Bladesmith's mark, enlarged 2/1. Inlaid in copper. Sword of Type XIIIa, early 14th century.

CHAPTER FIVE

Grip and Scabbard

THE basic ironwork of a sword needed certain perishable fittings to make it into a serviceable weapon. Such fittings rarely survive, as they were made of wood or horn, or leather, cord and textile materials. Nevertheless some have been preserved, enough to prove the reality of their existence, the methods of their making and the changes time wrought in their shape. This somewhat scanty archaeological evidence is supported by, and in its turn bears out, the evidence of art and literature.

These fittings were the grip and the scabbard—or to be more accurate, the grip and all the varying fittings which embellished, covered and completed it, and the scabbard and its varying mounts. The most important both in its essential purpose and the changes which fashion and the changing centuries brought about in its shape, is the grip. The scabbard, a fitting by no means essential to the sword itself, being simply a convenient case to carry it about in, is secondary.

Within the period 1100–1500 the grips of swords were of many different shapes, and were covered or embellished in different ways. Some of these variations may be attributed to the personal taste of a sword's owner, but others are clearly attributable to changes in fashion and so may give useful guidance in dating. First, the form and construction of the grip should be examined.

There was one basic manner of construction: the grip must consist of a hard core, of wood or bone or horn, covered with some form of membrane or bind-

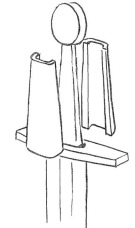

Fig. 109. "Sandwich" method of forming the grip.

129

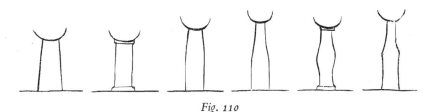

Fig. 110

ing. This of course was never a hard and fast rule, for there would have been exceptions, such as grips made of metal (as was common in the Viking period and the 18th century). In some cases a core of horn—even of wood—may have been left uncovered.

There were two ways of actually making the grip and fitting it to the tang. One was to make the wooden core in two flat halves, making as it were the two halves of a mould of which the object to be moulded was the tang (fig. 109). This method was generally used only when the tang was flat and broad, though there are examples extant where it is used on a narrow tang[1]. The other method, used over a narrow or stalk-like tang, is to form the grip's core by the use of a rasp, or by chiselling or whittling with a knife to the required shape, then boring a hole longitudinally down the centre. Then the grip is held firmly in a vice, the tang is heated in the furnace; and carefully pushed into the hole in the grip. Thus the hole is enlarged by the burning to the exact shape of the tang over which it is to fit. Care would have to be taken not to make the tang too hot, as this might split the wood of the grip or burn it too fiercely.[2] In the case of grip-cores of horn or ivory a more laborious process of filing may have been necessary.

Grips made in the "mould" method tend to be of a very flat oval section, while those made by the boring-through method are much more round in section, often circular or hexagonal. The different forms of grip may be loosely divided into those which are characteristic of swords of Group I, and those characteristic of Group II, but there was considerable overlapping (figs. 110, 111).

The "moulded" method was in use in the Viking period and continued into the 12th century. There were probably isolated instances of it much later, for there are swords of the 14th and 15th

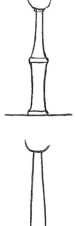

Fig. 111.

---

[1] As, for instance, the sword in the Library of Westminster Abbey.

[2] This method I have used myself in making swords; too much heat tends to destroy the grip.

centuries whose tangs are very broad, so broad that only a "mould" core could be used—even one like a sandwich in some cases. In the earlier period of the "mould" core's usage, c. 850–1200, it tended to be short (some 3″–3½″), rather broad at the cross (about 1¼″) tapering slightly and straightly to about ¾″ at the pommel. Characteristic of this shape is the sword (plate 2B) in the Musée de l'Armée in Paris, c. 1150, the so-called "Sword of St. Maurice" in Turin (c. 1200); and the later one (c. 1275–1300) in the Instituto del Conde de Valencia de Don Juan in Madrid (see plate 18).

The bored-through grips tended to swell slightly in the middle —like an extremely elongated barrel—though many were straight-sided. Some had small latitudinal flanges carved in the wood at top and bottom as in the surviving grips on the sword (c. 1300) on plate 46B, and another (c. 1470) on plate 46D.

With the advent of swords of Group II after c. 1350 new grip-styles appear, though the old ones continued in use. Most charac-teristic was the style which seems most usually to have been fitted to long-gripped swords. Although this characteristic form seems—on evidence so far available—to have been in use as early as about 1370, it did not become common until c. 1420; its greatest popu-larity seems to have been between c. 1450 and c. 1570. It is a shape difficult to describe, being almost dual in form. It is divided roughly in half by a latitudinal ridge; below this it is flat oval in section, tapers very slightly down to the cross, and its edges are slightly concave; above the midway rib it is a more circular section

Fig. 112. Effigy of Bishop Johannes von Eglofstein, Wurzburg Cathedral, 1411.

(though this may be hexagonal) and tapers like the neck of a bottle sharply towards the pommel (see figs. 112, 113).

Where the sword's grip was short there seem to have been three main varieties. One of these is the immemorial oval-section grip (it goes back to the time of the ancient Celtic peoples), swelling a little half-way up and tapering slightly towards the pommel. Another is one of almost circular section, swell-ing very strongly in the middle (figs. 75, 76 and plate 46D), and the third is characteristic only of a short period and

Fig. 114. Brass of Sir William Echyngham, Etchingham, Essex, c. 1430.

Fig. 113. Effigy of Johan Georg von Waldburg, Waldsee, c. 1470.

131

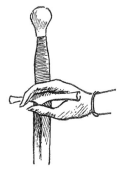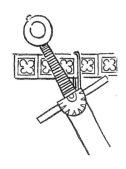

Fig. 115. From a relief over the north door of Karschau Cathedral, 1360–1400.

Fig. 116. From the Villa Pandolfini Frescoes, Farinata degli Uberti, by Andrea de Castagno, c. 1420.

Fig. 117. The sword of Joab, from the Velislav Bible, c. 1380.

is therefore by far the most interesting. This is shaped rather like a hock-bottle, and may be said to be an adaptation of the mid-ridged dual-shaped grip suitable for a sword with a short tang. First appearing in art (mostly upon English monumental brasses) (figs. 81, 82, 115 and 116) at about 1390, it is shown with great frequency until about 1430 (fig. 82), then disappears altogether. Actual examples are rare—in fact I only know of two where the grips can be regarded with reasonable certainty as being genuine[3] (plates 36A and 43B). There are one or two existing swords (plate 32 for example) where on a short tang there is a grip of the distinctive dual kind; but in art such grips are not shown on short-hilted swords.

While there seem to have been eight basic forms of grip in common use, the variety of methods by which they were covered and completed was probably infinite, for much would depend upon the fashion current in any given period and the individual taste of the owner. One should remember, too, that in the working life of a sword, its grip may have had to be re-bound or covered very many times, and during its lifetime any grip may have had literally dozens of coverings, all perhaps of a different kind. So the best that can be done is to give a few notes on what we can learn from art and surviving examples.

Literary references are scanty and unreliable since the only description, if it can be so called, is of "garnishing", a term which could apply to either the covering of the grip itself or to the "chappe". This chappe (meaning "cape") is a small flap of material

[3] See Oakeshott, *The Archaeology of Weapons*, op. cit., pp. 330–331.

which is fitted over the upper side of the cross between it and the bottom of the grip, and falls on each side of the central écusson of the cross to cover the opening of the scabbard mouth. This feature was by no means universally used, but there are many clear representations of it in art (as for instance in figs. 79, 80, 113, 115 and 117), and there are one or two notable survivals, i.e. the sword of Estore Visconti at Monza (plate 21 and p. 58), and the ceremonial sword of Frederic III in the Waffensammlung in Vienna (plate 42A and p. 126). A further example, hitherto un-noticed, is in a sword hilt—the blade is broken off 4″ below the cross—in the British Museum. This appears to have been Type XII, c. 1250, with a pommel of Type H and a cross of Style 2. It has been excavated (find-place unrecorded) but the chappe of leather remains.

An example of the typical reference to garnishing in inven-tories may be found in the inventory of the effects of Raoul de Nesle, Constable of France, who fell in the battle of Courtrai in 1302: "Item, a sword garnished with hide", and "Item, another

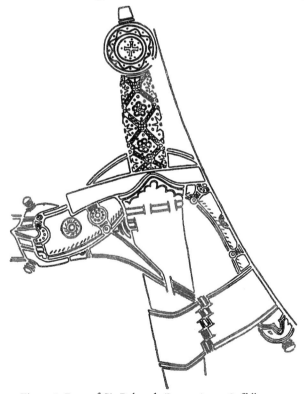

Fig. 118. Brass of Sir Robert de Bures, Acton, Suffolk, 1302.

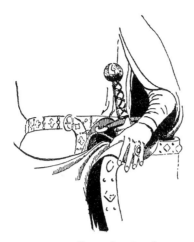

Fig. 119. Effigy of Wiprecht von Groitsch, Pegau, Saxony, c. 1230.

garnished with the arms of Nesle in needlework".[4] Such references could as well be applied to the chappe as to the grip.

However we are on much firmer ground when we examine the evidence of art. In manuscript pictures, monumental brasses and effigies and sculpture, very many styles of covering are shown. The commonest is a simple binding of cord or wire, but more decorative forms are shown as well, as for instance in the brass of Sir Robert de Bures (1302) at Acton, Suffolk (fig. 118), Sir Robert de Septvans (1306) at Chart, Kent (fig. 93), and countless effigies in England, Germany, Spain and Italy. These show more or less elaborate bindings of cord or wire, made basically in this fashion: the grip-core is bound with a narrow cord or wire, and upon this is superimposed another binding in coarser cord forming a diaper pattern over the basic binding. This diaper is made in the same way, and by using the same knots, as a string-bag is made (figs. 119, 120).

There are at present three surviving grips, dating between 1270 and 1330, which show very distinctly three different methods of making such grip-coverings. The first is the sword found in the tomb of Fernando de la Cerda (1270) in the chapel of the mona-stery of las Huelgas de Burgos[5] (plate 10), where in addition to the double binding each end of the grip is further embellished with a sort of circular tassel made of red silk cord—a feature very familiar in two-hand swords of the 16th century, and on many swords of 16th and 17th century date, but not usually expected upon the hilt of a 13th century one. The second of these surviving grips is on the sword found in the tomb of Can Grande della Scala, Lord of Verona (1329) now in the Museo Archaeologico of that city (see p. 38 and plate 46A). In this case the basic binding is of silver wire with a cord of green silk superimposed. The third example is the sword sometimes called "of Santa Casilda", pre-

---

[4] Burlington Magazine, VI, 468.

[5] Gomez–Moreno, Manuel, *El Panteon Real de las Huelgas de Burgos*, Madrid, 1946

served in the Instituto del Conde de Valencia de Don Juan in Madrid (see p. 124 and plate 18). Here the grip-core is covered with scarlet leather; over this a diaper of scarlet leather thonging is fastened with small gilt-headed pins.

The elaborate binding of the sword-hilt on the de Bures brass probably represents a basic binding of elaborately patterned needlework covered by a cord diaper. A monument dating about 1270 in the Stiftskirche in Stuttgart, to Count Ulrich von Wurttemberg, shows a grip which seems to be covered by closely plaited flat leather thongs—though it may be intended to represent plaited wire; a grip so covered was found in the Thorsbjerg bog in Denmark, a Roman weapon of the 2nd century A.D.; and of course this was a common method of binding grips in the 17th century, familiar to nearly everyone (fig. 121).

The grips of many swords were finished with a simple plain covering of leather, vellum or fabric, as for example the famous so-called "Sword of St. Maurice" in the Armeria Reale at Turin, where the grip is covered with plain vellum which shows upon it no marks of any superimposed binding. Such marks are quite plain, however, on a sword (plate 46B) of c. 1300 in my possession, where the blackened leather of the grip plainly shows the indentations of a spirally wound cord or thong. Such a binding is clearly seen on hilts in many 13th century sculptured figures in Germany (figs. 122a, 123).

The foregoing grips and the styles they represent are all on swords of Group I and date between 1100 and 1350. However, even though after 1350 new and distinctive styles of grip-covering developed, the old ones continued in use. During the late 14th and 15th centuries the plain binding of cord or wire became far more common, the diapered over-binding being rather rare. Where wire was used (as on the sword of Estore Visconti of 1413) it always seems to have been a twisted multi-strand wire. Sometimes, as on the grip of a later

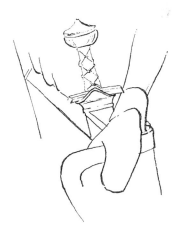

Fig. 120. St. Theodore, from the south porch of Chartres Cathedral, c. 1230.

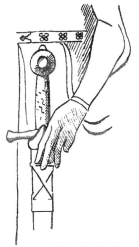

15th century sword (Frontispiece) in my possession, the diaper binding itself may be of twisted wire. In this case the grip core, covered with red velvet, has the lines carved in the wood where the crossed wires lie. The wires are double; a twisted silver wire lying alongside a plain steel one.

Some cord-bound grips were covered with a very thin membrane of leather, kid or doeskin being used as well as ordinary thin calf-skin. When this was done, the cord stands out a little through the overlying membrane, thus giving a slightly ridged quality to the grip. Many such grips survive, mostly dating be-

Fig. 121. Effigy of Ulrich von Wurttemberg. Stuttgart. Stiftskirche, c. 1260.

tween 1480–1550.

The long dual-shaped grips of the 15th century, particularly the second half of it, were often covered differently in each half. The lower might be covered with leather, while the upper is bound with wire (or vice-versa). Sometimes the upper part was made of solid metal. A good example of the first may be seen in the picture of St. Knut in the Trinity College Altarpiece in the collection of Her Majesty the Queen, now on loan to the National Gallery of

Fig. 122a. From a figure on the tomb of Bishop Siegfried von Eppstein, c. 1280.

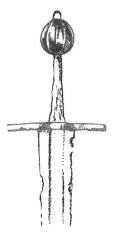

Fig. 122b. Sword in the Museum of Archaeology, Cambridge, cf. pommel of fig. 122a.

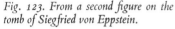
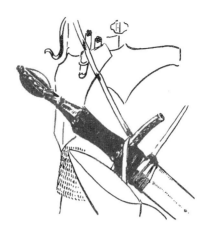

Fig. 123. From a second figure on the tomb of Siegfried von Eppstein.

Fig. 124. From the Trinity College Altarpiece, Edinburgh.

Scotland (fig. 124) painted in 1478-9. Here the lower part of the grip is embellished by little rosettes, six round the top end of the lower part, six round the bottom and one in middle of each face. Similar rosettes may be seen on the grip—an ordinary single-handed one—of the sword on the effigy of Sir Giles D'Aubeney (1502) in Westminster Abbey.

There is a "hock-bottle" grip in the Metropolitan Museum of Art in New York (plate 23) where there is no binding, but the core is supported (and the actual "grip" enhanced) by mounts of bronze-gilt. There are moulded collars below the pommel and above the cross, and each side of the grip—each edge, as it were—has a narrow strip of metal running from cross to pommel.

The foregoing notes refer only to a tiny minority of the grips once existing, and only describe a few of the survivors, but these few do seem to be typical of the styles in use during the age of chivalry.

The scabbard of a sword, though an essential fitting, cannot be taken as evidence of its sword's date whether it is an actual survivor or is depicted in art. Though it seems clear that medieval scabbards were stoutly constructed of durable materials, they would have been subjected to very hard wear, and during its working lifetime (which might have covered over a century) a sword would wear out many sheaths. Each time a new one was made, it is reasonable to assume that its mounting would have been in the latest fashion. Thus a sword, of, say, *c*. 1300 might well be in use in 1415 carried in a typical scabbard of the later period.

That fashion changed frequently, after *c*. 1300, in the style of scabbard mountings is clearly shown in art. Rather than waste space in making detailed comments on these variations of fashion, let the medieval artist do here what is best done by him anywhere: show for himself what sort of mounts were in use between *c*. 1100 and 1500 (figs. 16, 17, 21, 43, 70, 81, 82, 101, 117, 118, 120, 125).

Fig. 125. Sword from the R. Thames at Westminster, London Museum. The silver scabbard mounts are of a style fashionable between c. 1310–1340. Both blade and pommel bear the same smith's mark, made by the same punch.

Appendix:
Postscript to the 1994 Edition

SINCE the first edition of this book, material has come to light to provide evidence for some extension and amendment of this study. This material is in the form of several newly-found swords from the earth or rivers, and a few swords that have emerged into the light of examination after lurking hitherto unnoticed in private collections. The most important find is a group of eighty swords from the Dordogne river at Castillon la Bataille with a positive date for their loss at July 1453. In addition, the recent examination of unrecorded 11th and 12th century swords and their correlation with known ones has thrown fresh light upon blade inscriptions. It has also caused me to be certain that it is necessary to interpose a sub-type between Types X and XI (pp. 28–37), which should be called XA.

In characteristic, Type XA has a slightly longer blade than in Type X, yet generally shorter and broader than in Type XI. The most significant feature is that the fuller runs to within a few inches of the point, but is narrower than in Type X but wider than in Type XI, occupying one-third of the width of the blade. Hilts of most of these swords seem to have Brazil-nut pommels of Type A and rather long crosses of style 1, though some have disc pommels and rather stout crosses. Study of these swords confirms my belief that the well-known iron inlays of the Ingelrii and Gicelin groups, and those with the religious invocation INNOMINEDOMINI, are paralleled by contemporary inscriptions, often of a totally different character, delicately inlaid in silver. Many swords of Types X and XA have the "old" iron inlays, while similar ones (and when I say "similar" here I mean a peas-in-the-pod similarity, for to use the word "identical" in the case of any artefact of this kind is semantically inadmissible) have the "new" silver inlays. In short, the iron inlays are no more "old" than the silver ones are "new": they are contemporary.

The swords from the 1453 site are particularly interesting because they too show a feature which has generally not been accepted as possible. Of the eighty swords, many are as alike as nine peas in a pod, some of them seeming to have been mounted by the same hilt-maker. (The swords shown in plates 22A and 35A are of this kind.) These are certainly as much alike as any group of cavalry sabres of the English 1796 Regulation Pattern would be. The others, though of a totally different style, contain two sets of twins; twins which find exact parallels in English monuments of the 1430s and 1440s and in two well-known specimens (plate 36A and fig. 88). These facts reinforce and stabilise the belief that while medieval swords were not made to patterns in any "Regulation" manner, they did fall into clearly defined "families". These "families" may cut across the Types – the swords referred to above are a case in point, some being of Type XV and some of Type XVIII – but remain quite distinct as a family group. It might be tempting to use these families for typing, but it will not work: they have to be accommodated within and as part of the present typology.

Four other distinctive sword families appear, two in the second half of the 11th century, one in the late 14th, and one in the 15th. The first is among swords of Type X, as exemplified by the weapon shown on plate 2A; the second, of

Type XA sword with iron-inlaid inscriptions; found in the River Fyris, near Uppsala, c. 1000–1050.

139

Type XA, as in plate 2C; the third, in swords of Type XV and XVA (plate 27C); the fourth, the well-known sword of Henry V in Westminster Abbey (1422), gives a starting-point for dating; and the sword of the Archduke Philip the Handsome in Vienna (c.1490) an end. Here again, I must make use of the pea-pod analogy, for they are less than identical though much more than merely similar. There is of course one vast, rather vague "family" to which every medieval sword which does not conform to the pea-pod likeness belongs; this is why the family arrangement cannot be used for typing.

Another thing which the isolation of these families from the general mass suggests is that the medieval sword-cutler, and his customers, were as much affected by actual changes in fashion as were their descendants in the 18th century; but whereas the 18th century gentleman might, to conform with fashion, need to acquire a new small-sword every season, the medieval knight could go for years before his sword-hilt became démodé. It has been possible to give positive dates to undated works of art by identifying the fashion shown in clothes and armour, but much more work needs to be done before the same use can be made of swords.

Of the swords of 1453, all of the first "family" were quite short, while of the remaining ones many were long (Type XVIIIA); one was even longer with a hand-and-a-half hilt, two were two-handers; one had a 14th century inscribed blade making it a Type XVI, and one was 1 cm shorter than the average of the first nine, but appeared to be of small proportions, hence giving rise to the supposition, quite erroneous, that it was a weapon made for a boy. Examination of this sword led to a close scrutiny of the whole question of small swords, of which there are many examples surviving and many more shown in art. The inescapable conclusion is that they were in fact "knightly" weapons used in war as well as for civilian use when travelling: "Riding Swords" is a very apt name which has been coined for them. Thus, the sword belonging to the Infante Don Juan, son of Alfonso X of Castile, which I have said "is a boy's sword" (p. 49) is, in fact, not. There *are* little swords made for boys, but they are unmistakable because their hilts are too small for an adult hand, which is never the case with "Riding Swords" such as Don Juan's.

Since 1964 a great deal of very important work on early medieval swords has been done in the North by Dr. Anatoly Kirpichnikov of Leningrad and Dr. Jorma Leppaaho of Helsinki. Publication by these great scholars of a mass of Viking and post-Viking swords from Russian and Finnish finds has added enormously to our knowledge, and it is sad that limitation of space prevents a detailed inclusion of this work. However, the following notes and corrections to the original text may go some way towards an appreciation of this work.

p.20

Stephen's battle of Lincoln in 1141. Thus, several of the swords in this find, now shown to be of 12th century, not 14th century, date, could have been used in Stephen's battle of Lincoln in 1141.

A necessary revision of dating has come about owing to the publication of the sword-finds in Finnish graves of late Viking date (c.1000–1120) made by Dr. Jorma Leppaaho of Helsinki University, who not only found the swords but revealed many inlaid inscriptions on their blades by the use of x-ray photographs, infra-red light and other technological methods to show inscriptions which otherwise would have been totally invisible.

These findings were published in 1964 by Dr. Ella Kwikovski, in Jorma Leppaaho, *Späteisenzeitliche Waffen aus Finnland. Schwertinschriften und Waffenverzierung der 9–12 Jahrhunderts,* Helsinki 1964.

I only noticed them in 1981 having been shown the book by Dr. Martin of the Royal Armouries. What is revealed in it revolutionises all previous assumptions regarding the date of blade-inscriptions, and the subsequent amendments to this book are based upon Leppaaho's work, as a preliminary study.

So-called "Battlefield" finds are mostly quite useless for dating, unless (a) a given sword was found upon the actual, known *field* of a battle or (b) in a nearby river, pond or lake where pursuit is *known* to have taken place. But it needs to be near the field if it is to be reliable, here, because all through the Middle Ages swords – as they had been in Celtic, Migration and Viking times – were often deliberately thrown into rivers or lakes. Only very few have been found at known, used fords, or at points where fighting took place or, indeed, could have taken place. Such are the eighty swords dredged up from the River Dordogne in 1972 near Castillon la Bataille.

Fig. 1. This is not a XII, it's a Xa, dating c.1100. Its twin is in the Tower Armouries. (Sub-type Xa is one which later research and observation has shown to be necessary to the typology.)

p.22

Crosses. I am completely wrong here, or I was in 1963. Leppaaho's finds show conclusively that most of the cross-styles of the High Middle Ages were in use in Viking times, and as more examples come to light, this becomes more apparent.

p.28

I have now isolated the blades with narrower fullers into Type Xa.

p.29

The tangs are by no means always broad and flat. They are sometimes narrow, of square section. There's as much weight and metal in them. See Leppaaho for several illustrations of Viking grave finds. Pommels also may be of profiled disc section or even of faceted disc form. See Leppaaho, Taf. 28,1.

These remarks about Christian and non-Christian inscriptions are pretty valueless in the face of Leppaaho's finds. See Leppaaho, Taf. 3, 1 and 2.

Also the remarks about flat or plump Brazil-nut pommels are nonsense. Both sorts (Leppaaho again) were in use from c.950 until at least 1250.

p.31

Type XI. Remarks concerning the fuller running up into the tang. I've said this occurs "in later examples". Rubbish, you find it by at least 1050–1100.

The one with Anglo-Saxon runes is, alas, no longer in my collection. I swapped it years ago with the Glasgow Museum for the 15th century legharness I used to wear, now gone who knows where. The sword of course is in Glasgow in the Kelvingrove museum, and is illustrated and fully described in my *Records of the Medieval Sword* (1991), No. XI.8, p.61.

pp.33–4

Vienna Sword of St. Maurice. By comparison with some of Leppaaho's finds, the hilt should also be of the same date as the blade. I suggest that the gilding and the lettering, as well as the arms on the pommel, were added for Otto IV's coronation.

p.35

The Fornham battle site. This is rather nonsense, because nobody knows for certain where the battle was fought, within an area of at least about 8 square miles around Fornham. There were not many people involved, so the whole battlefield would have only been about the size of a football pitch; and nobody knows now precisely where, near Fornham, the sword was found. The only information is that "it was found while digging a ditch near Fornham". So it does not need to be a relic of the battle at all. Besides, there are two Fornhams (Fornham St Peter and Fornham All Saints) so this greatly enlarges the area of possibility.

These doubts are greatly strengthened by the fact that there are other marks on the blade which I did not mention – on the SES side, an open hand at the end of the fuller near the point, and on the reverse, in the same spot, a crozier. These marks are identical with marks on a mid 11th century sword found by Leppaaho in a Viking grave, on a sword with a hilt of Petersen's type (Wheeler's Type VI q.v. above) plated with silver and decorated in the Urnes or Runestone style of c.1000–50. So by reason of its shape and the affinity of its inscriptions to some found in 11th century graves in Finland, it is unlikely to date later than c.1075. See Leppaaho, Taf. 26.1, 33 and 36.

p.37

Type XII. "at the time of writing...etc." Now there are several Type XII swords which have to be dated into the 12th or even the 11th century, owing to the correlation of Leppaaho's finds with some Type XII's which have been considered to be of the 13th century.

The sword in Zurich, illustrated at fig. 14 on p.38, which has a typical XII blade and a hilt which is Type VII, now has to be put into its proper place in the 10th-11th century, owing to Leppaaho who shows parallel hilts from Viking graves (Taf. 2 and 3).

p.38

Inscriptions...between 1200–1350 should be amended to between 1050 and 1250. These inscriptions have been very fully examined and published in my *Records of the Medieval Sword*, Appendix B, pp. 253–260 and in the Catalogue of the 3rd Park Lane Arms Fair of 1986.

p.39

The Turin St. Maurice sword is a Xa. The hilt, both as to cross and pommel, is of a style much in use c.1070–1120. See Leppaaho, Taf. 3, 7, 29. Similarly the blade-marks are paralleled in style by the Finnish finds (Taf.29).

p.42

Type XIII-XIIIa. ... *ample and convincing evidence that both type and sub-types belong to the period c.1240–1350.* No. There is now equally convincing evidence, partly from Finland and partly from similar and analogous blade inlays which must be from the same workshop and are probably by the same *hand*, that this type was in fact in use at least by c.1150! I can't give the evidence in full here for lack of space, but soon all these findings about blade-inlays will be published.

There is a good deal of evidence, too, of a less reliable kind, that the big Type XIIIa swords with Brazil-nut pommels which I have dated c.1250 must, by analogous pommel and cross forms, be a century earlier. No, not *must*; but because a sword in Berlin *must*, they very probably are.

Incontrovertible evidence that the use of a long (7"–8") grip and a "wheel" pommel were in use in the Viking Age is given by a watercolour drawing (dated 1846 and owned by the Society of Antiquaries) of the grave-goods of a 10th century Viking tomb cleared at Claughton Hall in Lancashire.

p.44

Epées courts or *parvae ensis*. I think there is no doubt that these are not swords, normally rather short, of Types XIV and XV, but really little ones (often referred to in the past as boy's swords (wrong) and now as "Riding Swords" (right)). For example, the little one in the library of the Society of Antiquaries, the one on the effigy of Richard Beauchamp at Warwick, the Barcelona St. George, and the little ones from the Castillon find; and another recently found in Southern France, published in the Catalogue of the 10th Park Lane Arms Fair, 1993, figs. 9, 10 and 11.

p.49

Type XIIIa. See remarks in note to p.42.

Reference to plate 19A showing Wallace Collection sword which I have called XIIIb, c.1300. It's a Xa, and by analogy with at least two of Leppaaho's swords (Taf. 23, 24 and 27, 28) *could* be of 11th-12th century date.

I don't think it *is*, but I don't know why I don't. There's no reason in it; that it's a Xa certainly is the reason for it to be as early as that, for *Type* in no way determines *date*. Nor, on the other hand, does its excellent condition mean that it has to be late, for there are many 10th, 9th, 8th, 6th century swords – even the Lindholmgard Celtic Iron Age sword of c.300BC – which are in as good a condition, and have been published all over the place. (Elis Behmer, Heribert Seitz, Hoffmeger, Davidson *et al*. There are two swords among Dr. Leppaaho's finds in Finland with hilts of precisely the same shape and proportions as this one. See *Records of the Medieval Sword*, No. Xa1, p.37.

I have said the Toledo sword of Don Juan, El de Tarifa, is a boy's sword. I doubt it. It's a *parva ensis!*

p.50

Type XIIIb. Fig. 24. Very important sword because of the section, the shoulder, and the mark. It's an excavated sword, all gummed up together when I got it. The cross was broken across the middle, so I took it off and (!) lost it. It was in very bad condition, as is the pommel, eaten like a honeycomb. But the blade is good. No longer in my care. I don't know where it is, which is a great pity.

A superlative XIIIb has come to light recently. Now in a private collection, it is illustrated in *Records of the Medieval Sword*, No. XIIIb.2, p.111.

Plate 12A. This sword is reliably dated, as is Christensen's (which used to be Claude Blair's).

The one in the Royal Scottish is a case when it could very well date c.1150+. The little silver inlay (Is it OSO, SOS or S? I can't remember.) is of a type in use only, as far as I know, c.1050–1150.

p.52
Type XIV. Sword in New York, plate 16. This is an enormous weapon. The inscription seems to be etched, like the Sancho IV sword in Toledo.

p.53
Plate 19B. Still in my collection. Ultimately after my demise it will be in the Fitzwilliam Museum in Cambridge.

pp.58–9
Type XV. *...well preserved sword in the Wallace Collection ...* By its hilt and blade form it conforms very closely with the Castillon swords of my Group A, which date before 1453, but probably little more than a few years before if my theories, based largely upon the evidence of this find, that swords were made in bulk and supplied by contractors, will hold water. (They no longer will. See my article in the 10th Park Lane Arms Fair Catalogue, 1993.)

During the second quarter of the 15th century (perhaps earlier) a new blade-section appeared. No, it did not. It had "appeared" about a century earlier, if we take only the evidence of swords which have so far been noticed. If we take the evidence of countless spear and lance-heads dating from the Celtic Iron Age to the 14th century A.D., and great numbers of fine sword-blades of the La Tène periods, into account, it appeared some considerable time earlier. There are also reliable representations in art dating from the 11th-12th centuries.

p.60
Type XVa. *...particularly lovely sword (plate 24) in the Metropolitan Museum of Art in New York.* Maybe this is after all a beautiful dud. The extreme slenderness and length of the point of the blade may be one piece of evidence that it is. So, perhaps, might the patination?

p.72
Type XVIIIb. *...my own collection.* Now not so.

pp.73–4
Type XIX. Two of the Castillon swords are of this type. Each has a tapering blade which, unlike most of the XIXs which I have noted, has an acute point and a stiff mid-rib. Maybe they should be sub-typed as XIXa? Each has a short fuller, ⅓ of the blade width, in the upper quarter, flanked by two short fullers of the same general width and flattened edges as in a Ricasso. Each has traces of etched and gilded decoration in the central fuller.
These two swords (of my Castillon Group B) seem to have been made, both hilts and blades, by the same maker – or rather, the two blades by A, and each of the two hilts by B, for each hilt has an identical, unusual pommel of faceted pear-shape put on upside down.
These are of extreme interest, I believe, and more work needs to be done on them.

p.81
Tea-cosy pommel *...earlier origin and shorter term of popularity ...* No, not really. It simply is that when I wrote the book in the early '60s fewer swords with tea-cosy pommels had been found than those with Brazil-nut pommels. Finds from Russia and Finland published since then have redressed the balance a little. I think now that each began at about the same time and lasted as long

as the other. However, the proportion of surviving Brazil-nut-pommel swords to surviving tea-cosy-pommel ones is about 6–1, still.

p.82

...few of these swords among the Scandinavian finds. This is no longer true. There are stacks of them from all over the North, most of them out of graves.

Plate 1c. Now in the Glasgow Museum.

p.98

...the Korsoggaden sword, long believed to be of late Viking date, is in fact a Type XII, but *Type* has little to do with *date,* in swords within Group 1. The Runic experts (Erik Moltke and O. Rygh) who dated the runes c.1000–1050 were of course right; so was Petersen who dated it c.1050, followed by Hoffmeyer and everyone else except me.

The Cawood (or Clitheroe or Trent sword as some call it) has a hilt so exactly similar to the Korsoggaden one that they must come from the same shop, even the same hand. The Cawood sword is of course a XII, and because its hilt is of the same date as the Korsoggaden one, the sword too must date c.1050–1125.

There are three blade inscriptions which are so closely akin to the unusual style of the Cawood swords that they are probably by the same hand and so of the same date. This evidence is published in *Records of the Medieval Sword,* pp. 77–83.

The fact that the Korsoggaden sword was found in a stone cist (*not* a coffin – too small) with remains of its scabbard (a fact which I was unaware of, as was Hilda Davidson in *The Sword in Anglo-Saxon England*) is pretty clear evidence that, in the manner of the Vikings, it was buried carefully in a stone box, for preservation. See Hilda Davidson, *op. cit.* pp. 79–80.

This sword, the Cawood one, and the comparably inscribed ones, have changed some previously firmly held opinions on dating.

pp.98–9

...a so-called Viking sword in the British Museum ... Not "so-called" at all. It is a Viking sword, Petersen's hilt type 2, my type Xa, c.1000–1050.

The inscription on the blade ANTANATANAN is very small in silver letters, each one perfectly formed, and it is paralleled by a sword c.1100 in the Kunstgewerbemuseum in Düsseldorf which has a long Latin inscription on each side of the blade, in letters of the same style and size as the Canwick sword, and without much possibility of doubt by the same hand: QUIFALSITATEIVIVIT ANIMAMIOCCIDITIFALSUSIINIOREICARETIHONORE and QUIIESIHILARISIDATORI HUNCIAMATISALVATORIOMNISIAVARUSINULLIIESTICARUS. Correctly spelt, too. This is a pair of aphorisms from a moralistic treatise written c.1020–5 by Wipo of Burgundy as instruction for the son of the Emperor Konrad II (who later became Heinrich III).

So the analogy of the Düsseldorf sword's inlays with those of the Canwick sword, the fact that the Canwick sword is a Viking one, and that Wipo's aphorisms were in popular circulation (*how* popular?) c.1030–1100 all tends to suggest a date for both swords.

The hilt of the Canwick sword is exactly matched by one from Finland (Leppaaho, Taf. 37) and the Düsseldorf one by another (*ibid.,* Taf. 12, 25, 26). The Düsseldorf sword is illustrated in Hoffmeyer, Vol. II, plate Xe.

p.103
Pommel type Ii. ...*earliest datable example*... etc. Now the earliest examples are from Leppaaho's Finnish Viking graves, c.1050–1100. See Leppaaho, Taf. 28.1 and 43.

p.105
Pommel type T2. ...*found in the River Cam*. No. Found in the Great Ouse at Ely. Fully described in *Records of the Medieval Sword*, No. XVII.1, pp.158–9 and I have said elsewhere that "the sword is particularly big". It is not. Its blade is 36" long, and is light and beautifully balanced. An exquisite sword to wield.

p.107
Pommel type V. *There are few examples*... Not now. So far there are in circulation six from the Castillon find, with who knows how many more among the eighty swords in the hoard. They *must* have been in a wagon? They were not. They were in a *cask*, in a sunken barge. The sword mentioned as being in my collection is there no longer.

p.109
Pommel type V2. *Four examples survive*. Now, in 1994, there are several more from the Castillon find.

p.114
Cross style 2. Two of these styles of cross were found on 11th century swords in Finland. See Leppaaho, Taf. 23,2 and 28,2.
Cross style 3. *Popular during the period c.1150–1250*. Amend to c.1050–1200 (Leppaaho again).
Cross style 4. These crosses are quite often found on swords dating c.1050–1120, e.g. one in a private collection in Northumberland (not published, but there is a photograph in *Records of the Medieval Sword* and I have examined it. There are the remains of an INNOMINE inscription in the blade.) and one in the Kienbusch collection in the Art Museum in Philadelphia. The remarks I made above regarding the difficulty of forging pommels also apply to crosses. Very often the shape of a cross – whether it is straight or curved in various degrees – may well have come about of its own accord during the forging process.

p.119
Back-edged sword in Rome (plate 43A) "of a pattern distinctive of the years between c.1275 and 1325." I am not so sure now, since Leppaaho. It could go back (does, as a style) to c.1050. The roundel mark appears on one of Leppaaho's 12th century blades.

p.130
Footnote 1. This grip of the Henry V sword is a horrid, crude late replacement (a sandwich) perhaps as old as the 18th century. Looks as if it was hacked out of a bit of oak with a penknife. *Not* the original, which would have got very fragile with age and dust if not actually rotted off.

p.135
Wire binding of grips. Plenty of evidence of Viking swords' grips bound with wire, twisted or plain. There are remains of plain brass wire on the surviving grip of one of the Castillon swords, a two-hander (in the Royal Armoury).

Bibliography

Among the vast number of books which treat of armour and weapons, there are only two dealing specifically with the sword in medieval Europe; and though there are passing references to and illustrations of these weapons in most publications concerned with arms (other than firearms), and many articles have appeared during the last seventy-five years which deal with them, there can be no list of books for further reference. The only sources of information are those used by the author: countless medieval manuscripts and sculptures, and the paintings of the 15th century. A list is appended, however, of some among the many publications which provide easily accessible reproductions of sculpture and painting, together with those works on armour which are of positive value in this study.

ACTA ARCHAEOLOGICA UNIVERSITATIS LODZENSIS: NO. 3. NADOLSKI, ANDREJ, "Studia nad Uzbrojeniem Polskim W. x, xi, i xii Wieku". Lodz, 1954.

BEHMER, ELIS. *Das Zweischneidige Schwert der Germanische Völkerwänderungszeit*, Stockholm, 1939.

BLAIR, CLAUDE. *European Armour*, Batsford, 1958.
    Weapons in Europe and America, Batsford, 1962.

BRUHN, HOFFMEYER, ADA. *Middelalderens Tvaeeggede Sverd*, Copenhagen, 1954.

CODEX, MANESSE. Ms. facsimile, Leipzig, 1925–27.

CRIPPS DAY, F. H. *Fragmenta Armamentaria*. 6 vols. Privately printed. Frome and London, 1934–56.

CROSSLEY, A. H. *English Church Monuments, 1150–1550*. 1921.

DEHIO, G. and BEZOLD, G. V. *Die Denkmäler der deutschen Bildauerkunst*. 3 vols. Berlin, 1905.

EVANS, JOAN. *Medieval Art in France*, Oxford University Press, 1943.

FFOULKES, C. J. *The Armourer and His Craft from the 11th to the 15th Century*. London, 1912.

FREYHAN, F. *Die Illustrationen zum Casseler Willehalms Codex*, Marburg, 1928.

FRYER, A. C. *Wooden Monumental Effigies.* 1924.
    Medieval Sculpture in France, 1931.

GARDNER, A. *Alabaster Tombs.* Cambridge, 1940.

GAY, VICTOR. *Glossaire Archéologique.* Paris, 1887.

GIORGETTI, G. *Armi Bianchi*, Associazione Amatori Armi Antichi, San Marino, 1961.

GOLDSCHMIDT, A. *Die Skulpturen von Freiburg und Wechselburg.* 1924.

HAMANN, R. *Die Elizabethskirche zu Marburg* (vol. II, 'Die Sculpturen'), Marburg, 1929.

HARMAND, ADRIEN. *Jeanne d'Arc: Ses Coutumes, Son Armure. Essai de Reconstruction.* Paris, 1929.

HEWITT, JOHN. *Ancient Armour and Weapons in Europe.* 3 vols. London and Oxford, 1855–60.

JAMES, M. R. *The Romance of Alexander*, a collotype facsimile of MS. Bodley 264, Oxford, 1935.

KELLY, F. M. and SCHWABE, RUDOLPH. *A Short History of Costume and Armour. 1066–1800.* 2 vols. London, 1931.

KUEAS, H. *Die Naumburger Werkstatt*, 1937.

The Kretschmar von Kienbusch Collection of Armor and Arms, Princeton University, 1963.

LAKING, SIR G. F. *A Record of European Armour and Arms through Seven Ages.* 5 vols. London, 1920–22.

MANN, SIR JAMES. Wallace Collection Catalogue, European Arms and Armour. 2 vols. London, 1962.

OAKESHOTT, R. EWART. *The Archaeology of Weapons.* London, 1960.

PETERSEN, JAN. *Die Norske Vikingesverd*, 1919.

PRIOR, E. S. and GARDNER, A. *An Account of Medieval Figure Sculpture in England.* Cambridge, 1921.

SZENDREI, J. *Ungarische Kriegsgeschichtlicher Denkmaler*, Budapest, 1896.

THOMAS, BRUNO. *Deutsche Plattnerkunst.* Munich, 1944.

THOMAS, B. and GAMBER, O. *Die Innsbrucker Plattnerkunst.* Innsbruck, 1954.

THORDEMANN, BENGT. *Armour from the Battle of Visby* (in English). Stockholm, 1939.

TRAPP, OSWARD GRAF, and MANN, (SIR) J. G. *The Armoury of the Castle of Churburg.* London, 1929.

VALENCIA, CONDE DE. Catalogo Historico-descriptivo de la Real Armeria de Madrid. Madrid, 1898.

VAN MARLE, RAIMOND. *The Italian Schools of Painting*, 14 vols. The Hague, 1931.

WHEELER, R. E. M. *London and the Vikings*, London Museum Catalogue, 1927.

Index